CAMBRIDGE LIBRARY COLLECTION

Books of enduring scholarly value

Travel and Exploration

The history of travel writing dates back to the Bible, Caesar, the Vikings and the Crusaders, and its many themes include war, trade, science and recreation. Explorers from Columbus to Cook charted lands not previously visited by Western travellers, and were followed by merchants, missionaries, and colonists, who wrote accounts of their experiences. The development of steam power in the nineteenth century provided opportunities for increasing numbers of 'ordinary' people to travel further, more economically, and more safely, and resulted in great enthusiasm for travel writing among the reading public. Works included in this series range from first-hand descriptions of previously unrecorded places, to literary accounts of the strange habits of foreigners, to examples of the burgeoning numbers of guidebooks produced to satisfy the needs of a new kind of traveller - the tourist.

Voyages of the Venetian Brothers, Nicolo & Antonio Zeno

The publications of the Hakluyt Society (founded in 1846) made available edited (and sometimes translated) early accounts of exploration. The first series, which ran from 1847 to 1899, consists of 100 books containing published or previously unpublished works by authors from Christopher Columbus to Sir Francis Drake, and covering voyages to the New World, to China and Japan, to Russia and to Africa and India. Nicolò (c. 1326–1402) and Antonio Zeno (died c. 1403) were navigators from Venice. In 1558 a descendant of Nicolò Zeno published a series of letters between the brothers purporting to show voyages of exploration undertaken in the north Atlantic and North America between 1390 and 1400. These letters are controversial and considered to be forgeries, as contemporary records place Nicolò Zeno in Venice during this period. However R.H. Major provides a sympathetic analysis of this material, demonstrating the ingenuity of this fabricated account.

T0370832

Cambridge University Press has long been a pioneer in the reissuing of out-of-print titles from its own backlist, producing digital reprints of books that are still sought after by scholars and students but could not be reprinted economically using traditional technology. The Cambridge Library Collection extends this activity to a wider range of books which are still of importance to researchers and professionals, either for the source material they contain, or as landmarks in the history of their academic discipline.

Drawing from the world-renowned collections in the Cambridge University Library, and guided by the advice of experts in each subject area, Cambridge University Press is using state-of-the-art scanning machines in its own Printing House to capture the content of each book selected for inclusion. The files are processed to give a consistently clear, crisp image, and the books finished to the high quality standard for which the Press is recognised around the world. The latest print-on-demand technology ensures that the books will remain available indefinitely, and that orders for single or multiple copies can quickly be supplied.

The Cambridge Library Collection will bring back to life books of enduring scholarly value (including out-of-copyright works originally issued by other publishers) across a wide range of disciplines in the humanities and social sciences and in science and technology.

Voyages of the Venetian Brothers, Nicolo & Antonio Zeno

To the Northern Seas, in the XIVth Century

EDITED BY RICHARD HENRY MAJOR

CAMBRIDGE UNIVERSITY PRESS

Cambridge, New York, Melbourne, Madrid, Cape Town, Singapore,
São Paolo, Delhi, Dubai, Tokyo

Published in the United States of America by Cambridge University Press, New York

www.cambridge.org
Information on this title: www.cambridge.org/9781108011402

This edition first published 1873
This digitally printed version 2010

ISBN 978-1-108-01140-2 Paperback

WORKS ISSUED BY

The Hakluyt Society.

———◆———

THE VOYAGES OF
NICOLÒ AND ANTONIO ZENO.

M.DCCC.LXXIII.

THE

VOYAGES

OF THE VENETIAN BROTHERS,

NICOLÒ & ANTONIO ZENO,

TO THE NORTHERN SEAS,

IN THE XIVTH CENTURY,

COMPRISING

THE LATEST KNOWN ACCOUNTS OF

THE LOST COLONY OF GREENLAND;

AND OF

THE NORTHMEN IN AMERICA

BEFORE COLUMBUS.

TRANSLATED AND EDITED,

WITH NOTES AND AN INTRODUCTION,

BY

RICHARD HENRY MAJOR, F.S.A., &c.

LONDON:

PRINTED FOR THE HAKLUYT SOCIETY.

M.DCCC.LXXIII.

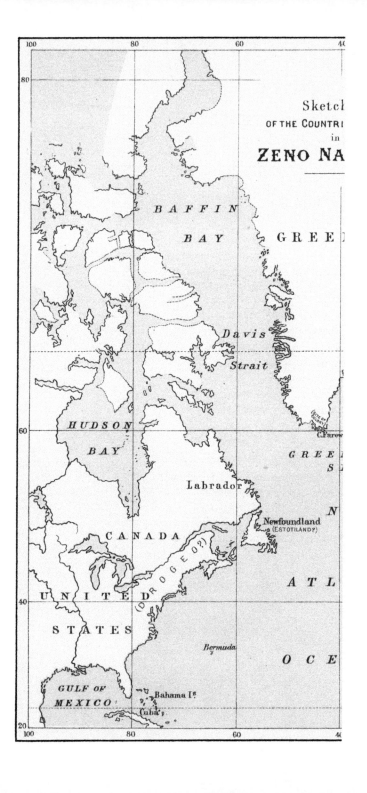

Sketch
OF THE COUNTRI...
in
ZENO NA...

BAFFIN

BAY

GREE...

Davis

Strait

GREE...
S...

C.Farew...

HUDSON

BAY

Labrador

Newfoundland
(ESTOTILAND?)

N...

CANADA

(DROGEO?)

ATL...

UNITED

STATES

Bermuda

OCE...

GULF OF
MEXICO

Bahama Is

Cuba

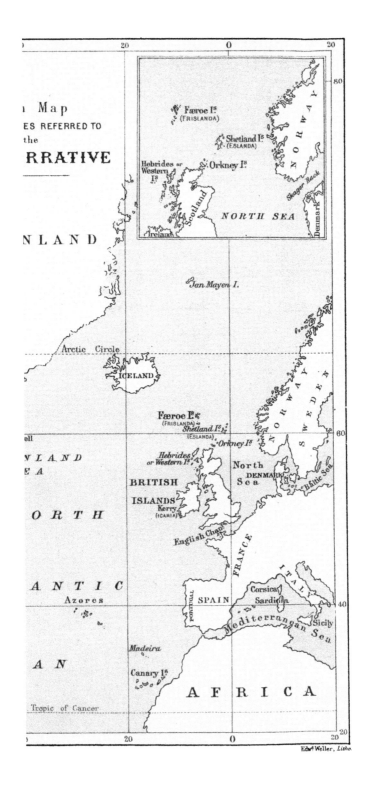

20 0 20

1 Map
ES REFERRED TO
the
RRATIVE

80

Færoe Iˢ
(FRISLANDA)

Shetland Iˢ
(ESLANDA)

Hebrides or
Western
Iˢ

Orkney Iˢ

N O R W A Y

Scotland

Skager Rack

Denmark

N O R T H   S E A

Ireland

N L A N D

Jan Mayen I.

Arctic Circle

ICELAND

N O R W A Y

S W E D E N

Færoe Iˢ
(FRISLANDA)

Shetland Iˢ
(ESLANDA)

Orkney Iˢ

60

ell

N L A N D
E A

Hebrides
or Western Iˢ

North
Sea

DENMARK

Baltic Sea

BRITISH

O R T H

ISLANDS
Kerry
(ICARIA)

English Chan

FRANCE

ITALY

A N T I C
Azores

PORTUGAL SPAIN

Corsica
Sardinia

40

A N

Madeira

Mediterranean Sea

Sicily

Canary Iˢ

A F R I C A

Tropic of Cancer

20

20 0 20

PREFACE.

THE nucleus of this small volume is, in respect of quantity, remarkably small; but the material which envelopes it and which supplies it with bulk enough to constitute a volume, is devoted to the purpose of showing that, if small in quantity, it is far from being insignificant in quality.

The very object of our Society being to deal with the Geography of the Past, by printing rare or unpublished ancient texts of travels, it is clearly a duty in Editors to supply their readers with full information as to the position, in regard both of time and importance, which the documents that they produce occupy, or ought to occupy, in the history of Geography. But it is equally clear that the proportion which the illustrative matter may bear to the extent of the original text, must vary very much according to the circumstances of each case. In the present instance, we have the peculiar phenomenon of a most true and authentic narrative, which must henceforth,

b

it is hoped, hold a high position among ancient historical records of travel, having been, in conjunction
with the map that accompanies it, the cause of a vast
amount of error and misconception, and the subject of
so much discredit as to have been finally condemned
as "false" and "a tissue of fiction." To track the causes
of such misconceptions and to free the document, if
possible, from the discredit under which it laboured,
became my duty as Editor. That I have succeeded
in so doing will, I trust, be acknowledged not as a
matter of opinion only, but of unanswerable fact. I
advert to that fact here solely with the view of ex-
plaining why the illustrative matter in the volume
should be so large in comparison with the text.

R. H. M.

INTRODUCTION.

THE duties of an Editor of one of our Hakluyt volumes are almost always limited to the elucidation of a text, which though antiquarian and therefore demanding a peculiar kind of editorial care, is at least undisputed as to its authenticity. Such is not the case in the present instance. By far the hardest portion of the task of preparing this introduction has been the investigation of the perplexities which hang about the Zeno narrative and the map which accompanies it. It was truly said by the learned John Pinkerton in his History of Scotland (vol. i, page 261, Note) "Zeno's book is one of the most puzzling in the whole circle of literature." Unfortunately this perplexity, which up to the present time has baffled every commentator, has produced the mischievous but not unnatural effect of throwing discredit on the authenticity of a genuine and valuable narrative. It may even be said that this unlucky document has met with almost as injurious treatment from its advocates as from its enemies; since, from failing to detect the real solution of that which perplexed them, even friendly critics have been compelled to resort to random speculations, which have only "made confusion worse confounded." The puzzle consisted in this,

that it presented geographical information very far
in advance not only of what was known by geographers in the fourteenth century, when the narrative
was first written, but greatly in advance also of the
geography of the sixteenth century, when it was
published. At the same time the narrative, and the
map which accompanied it, contained names of places
which in the form of their spelling and the positions
assigned to them, were so irreconcileable with all
that geographers have been able to learn from other
sources, that they have given rise to the wildest conjectures, have puzzled the patient out of their wits,
and driven the impatient to condemn the whole
thing as an imposture. The story in brief is as
follows :—

Towards the close of the fourteenth century Nicolò
Zeno, a member of one of the noblest and most ancient
families in Venice, went, at his own expense, on a voyage rather of curiosity than discovery into the northern
seas. For a long series of years before his time the
Flanders voyage from Venice had been a matter of
almost annual occurrence, but chance gave to this
voyage a very peculiar interest. Nicolò Zeno was
wrecked on what he describes as the Island of Frislanda, which will presently be shown to be the Færoe
Group, and he and his companions were rescued
from the wreckers by the chief of a neighbouring
principality, named Zichmni, who happened to be
there, and into whose service he entered in the capacity of pilot of his fleet. After remaining with this
chieftain some time, during which is recorded the

conquest of Frislanda by Zichmni, Nicolò Zeno wrote
home to his brother Antonio, inviting him to join
him, which he did. Nicolò survived his brother's
arrival four years, and died in Frislanda. Antonio
remained ten years more in the service of Zichmni,
and then returned to Venice, where he died. It is
from the above-mentioned letter of Nicolò to Antonio
and subsequent letters from Antonio to a third
brother Carlo (a very distinguished man in Venetian
history) that the narrative of the movements of the
two brothers is derived. After Antonio's arrival the
two brothers accompanied Zichmni in a victorious
attack on what can be clearly shown to be the Shetland group, although named Eslanda. The narrative,
however, fortunately treats at greater length on two
much more important subjects ; viz., a visit by
Nicolò Zeno to Greenland, which he calls Engroneland, and the observations of some fishermen in two
parts of North America, called respectively Estotiland and Drogeo, showing the existence at that period,
more than a century before the time of Columbus, of
the remains of those old Scandinavian colonists mentioned by Adam of Bremen in the eleventh and
Ordericus Vitalis in the twelfth century, and about
whom we have learned so much in the present century from the Danish antiquaries C. C. Rafn and
others. The whole story had been written out by
Antonio Zeno, but a descendant of his, named Nicolò
Zeno, born in 1515, when a boy, not knowing the
value of these papers, tore them up, but, some of
the letters surviving, he was able from them subse-

quently to compile the narrative and publish it, as
we now have it, in the year 1558. He found also
in the palace a map, rotten with age, illustrative of
the voyages. Of this he made a copy, unluckily
supplying, from his own reading of the narrative,
what he thought was requisite for its illustration.
The first to do himself honour by vindicating the truth
of the Zeno story, was the distinguished companion
of Captain Cook, Johann Reinhold Forster, in his
"History of the voyages and discoveries in the North,"
published in *German*, Frankfort, 1784, *English*, London, 1786, 4to ; but the value of his dissertation is
marred by many wild conjectures. Eggers, in his well-
known prize essay on the True Site of the Old East
Greenland, Kiel, 1794, 8vo, was another advocate of
the truth of the narrative. Early in this century Cardinal Zurla wrote a lengthy work in favour of the voyages, but was so far from realizing the fact that the
Frislanda of the Zeno was the Færöe Islands, as is
plainly demonstrable from internal evidence, that he
concluded that it represented some island since sub-
merged. Zach, Buache, Malte Brun, Walckenaer, de la
Roquette, and the Polish geographer Joachim Le-
lewel, have all been advocates of the narrative.
In 1845, the Danish antiquary J. H. Bredsdorff
wrote a valuable paper on the subject in the third
volume of " Grönlands Historiske Mindesmaerker",
and has been more accurate and judicious than any
of his predecessors in his conjectures and commen-
taries on difficult points. But what is wanted is not
conjecture but demonstration, and Bredsdorff, in

common with all the rest, has failed in detecting those simple facts connected with the history of the document which would have led to inevitable conclusions in its favour. The deniers of the authenticity of the document have been numerous, and even so late as the present year, the distinguished Professor Konrad Maurer has printed his opinion that the Zeno narrative is a compilation of Nicolò Zeno Junior's from a variety of sources. But of all those who have thrown discredit upon the document, the most conspicuous is Admiral Zahrtmann, the late hydrographer to the Danish Admiralty, who in the year 1836 published in the fifth volume of the Journal of the Royal Geographical Society, an article of the most learned and elaborate character translated from the Danish, the object of which is to prove that the whole story is "false" and "a tissue of fiction", emanating from the pen of Nicolò Zeno junior in 1558. It was said with great truth by a writer in the "North American Review" for July, 1838, after speaking of the various distinguished persons who have disputed or vindicated the credibility of this narrative :—" The most formidable assailant of the Venetian title to the discovery of the New World, is yet to be named. The essay of Captain Zahrtmann of the Danish navy, originally published in the transactions of the Royal Antiquarian Society of Copenhagen in 1833, and subsequently communicated to the London Geographical Society, is by far the ablest attempt ever made to shake the authority of the voyages of the Zeni. We must say that our first impressions after perusing that masterly production, were so strong against even the possible truth of the account, that we well nigh resolved to abandon the matter as beyond all hope of surgery without bestowing another thought upon it. The writer brings such a mass of *primâ facie* proof to bear upon the subject, and discovers so many loose points and apparent inconsistencies in the story, that the argument comes upon one with the force of demonstration. At the same time, the perfect freedom of the paper from vituperative remark, and the admirable coolness as well as skill with which the operator dissects his victim, are far from diminishing the effect produced upon the mind. A more careful examination, however, of this elaborate effort from the pen of so profound a scholar has suggested several ideas that detract, to some extent, from the conclusive character of the argument, and leave a ray of hope to the sanguine admirers of Venetian prowess." The Editor trusts that, if the reader will be pleased to follow him through this introduction, it will be found that this "ray of hope" has now expanded into noon-day light. The result of his investigation has been to prove Admiral Zahrtmann, either in his facts or his deductions, wrong on every point, and to convict him of throwing upon an honorable man, occupying no less distinguished a position than that of one of the Council of Ten of the Republic of Venice, a series of aspersions of the most ungenerous character. The "North American" reviewer just quoted, commends Admiral Zahrtmann for refraining from vituperative remark. "False-

hood" and "tissue of fiction" applied to different parts
of the narrative, are tolerably strong expressions; but,
if true, would be justifiable in criticism. How
different was the verdict of the illustrious and
far-seeing Humboldt, who, with his usual large-
mindedness, although he had perceived the difficulties
attaching to the narrative of the Zeni, said " On y
trouve de la candeur et des descriptions détaillées
d'objets, dont rien en l'Europe ne pouvoit leur avoir
donné l'idée" (*Examen Critique*, tom. ii, p. 122).
It is quite true that the complications and difficulties which surround this narrative are such as amply
to justify very serious doubts in the minds of those
who have never made a special analysis of the subject. Admiral Zahrtmann, however, *has* devoted
very special attention to such an analysis, and yet
has failed to perceive the facts which should have
averted such opprobrious epithets.

Not the least important of these, as will be presently
seen, is, that in order to fix localities which have been
written down by a southerner from the lips of northerners, it is requisite to follow strictly the narrative,
and see what names of places on the route tally, *not
in form, but in sound*, with those which have been
written down. This has never been done.

Admiral Zahrtmann summarizes his examination
of the subject into the four following conclusions :—

1. " That there never existed an Island of Frisland, but
that what has been represented by that name in the chart
of the Zeni is the Færoe Islands.

2. " That the said chart has been compiled from hearsay

information, and not by any seaman who had himself navigated in these seas for several years.

3. "That the 'History of the Voyages of the Zeni', more particularly that part of it which relates to Nicolò, is so replete with fiction, that it cannot be looked to for any information whatever as to the state of the north at that time.

4. "That both the history and the chart were most probably compiled by Nicolò Zeno, a descendant of the Zeni, who, for brevity's sake, may be called Nicolò Zeno, Junior, from accounts which came to Italy in the middle of the sixteenth century, being the epoch when information respecting Greenland first reached that country, and when interest was awakened for the colony which had disappeared."

These propositions and the arguments on which they are based, the Editor proposes to deal with in such order as shall seem to him best calculated to bring the series of details clearly before the reader's mind, and he will commence by transcribing the first proposition and its arguments *en bloc* just as they emanate from Admiral Zahrtmann's pen. The proposition stands thus :

1st. "That there never existed an Island of Frisland, but that what has been represented by that name in the chart of the Zeni is the Feroe Islands."

And the following is Admiral Zahrtmann's argument :

1. "The first point has already been proved by Buache, Eggers, and Malte Brun, by arguments which I shall not repeat, nor shall I relate the voyage itself,—a task already performed by various others. I shall only add a few remarks on the subject.

"Of the identity of Denmark, Norway, Sweden, and Scotland, there can be no doubt ; as not only their relative positions, their outlines, and the names of many places in them, but also their proper names in Latin, are decisive proofs of this. Of the five groups, Greenland, Iceland, Shetland, the Feröe Islands, and the Orkneys, we recognise the proper names of the three which end in ' land' ; whereas the two last, called in those days Fær-eyar and Orkneyar, are not to be found, these sounds being difficult to Italianise, or even to be at all caught or retained by any Italian ear. The name Gronlandia is applied, it is true, to quite a wrong place, where no land is to be found ; but that the Engroneland in the chart, which in Antonio Zeno's account is moreover called Gronlandia, corresponds with the present Greenland, is proved so evidently by its shape, that I cannot conceive how Eggers could entertain a moment's doubt on the subject, or could believe that it was land on the opposite side of Baffin's Bay ; the more so, as it is now ascertained that in that bay there is no St. James's Island in existence. The identity of Iceland is proved not only by the name Islanda, but further by the names of the bishop's sees, Scalodin and Olensis ; that these two names in particular should be so easily recognised, and should bear so close a resemblance to the Latin names of the places, seems to indicate that the accounts respecting them were drawn from ecclesiastical sources. Though Shetland is called Estland, yet, in the first place, this is only a trifling transposition of the name in the spirit of the Italian language, and not exhibiting any greater deviation than is found in the other appellations given at different times to these islands,—such as Hialtland, Yealtaland, Yetland, Zetlend, and Hetland ; and besides, we recognise so many names here that we are almost tempted to believe that this was precisely the part of the chart best known to the author. We find, for example, Cledere, i.e., Queendal, Sumbercouit (Sumbergh Head), St. Magnus (St. Magnus Bay), Scaluogi (Scalloway), Bristund (Brassa Sound), Itlant (Fetlar), Lonibies (Lambness), Onlefort (Olna-Firth), and Oloford (Onge-Firth). And further, the placing of St. Magnus and Scalloway on the east side instead of the west side, naturally leads to the inference that these names were not copied from any other chart, but laid down from verbal depositions. These points being admitted, the Orkneys must naturally be looked for between Shetland and Scotland; and this Eggers has done, but in my opinion, not in a very satisfactory manner. He supposes that the name Contanis may be assumed as Continent, or, in other words, Mainland, the largest of the Orkneys. I, on the other hand, consider beyond all doubt that it means Caithness (formerly called Katanes), the most northern county in Scotland, a province which, from the evidence of the ancient code of laws called the Grágás, we know belonged, in the middle ages, to the Crown of Norway. The only name I find to have a resemblance to any name in the Orkneys is Podalida, not unlike Pomonia, the principal island in the Orkneys, or Pentland (formerly Petland), the name of the strait which separates them from Caithness. Podalida corresponds with Pomonia in this respect also, that it is represented as a large island, surrounded by several smaller ones. This, however, is not quite satisfactory; we have, therefore, two groups remaining unaccounted for, viz., the Orkneys and the Feröe Islands, one of which must of necessity be Frisland : unless we would suppose that a seaman, who had for several years navigated the northern sea in all directions, should have remained ignorant of the existence of the Orkneys and the Feröe Islands, and at the same time known and laid down a country which has since disappeared, and of which, moreover, all the inhabitants of the north in those ages had ever remained in utter ignorance; this appears to me so very highly improbable, that we may safely pronounce it to be impossible. If we subsequently compare names and positions, we shall find that Frisland can be nothing else than the Feröe Islands; as the Rock Monaco, at the southern point, exactly corresponds to the position of the Rock Munk, in respect to the Feröe Islands, as the names Sudero Colfo, Streme, and Andefard must of necessity be considered homonymous with Suderö Sound, Strömöe, and Andefer; and, finally, as the absolute geographical position of Fris-

land corresponds better to that of the Feröe Islands, than
is the case with almost any of those places on the chart
concerning the identity of which no doubt can be entertained. The south end of Frisland, for example, is placed
in the latitude of the Feröe Islands, whereas the northern
extremity of Scotland is placed 2°, and all places in Greenland, Iceland, Shetland, Norway, and Denmark, are placed
about 6° too far northward. In like manner, the eastern
extremity of Frisland is laid down exactly as much to the
westward of the Naze as the western extremity of the Feröe
Islands is distant from that point; whereas Iceland is placed
10°, and Cape Farewell 20° of longitude nearer to the Naze
than they really are. This was, therefore, the place which
Antonio Zeno, who knew as little about Frisland as we
do, would, according to his brother's description, be
most likely to fall in with when he went in search of him.
It is further mentioned that Estland (Shetland) lies between
Frisland and Norway, which is its relative position to the
Feröe Islands; and, finally, it is expressly stated that Frisland was subject to the King of Norway; but as we know
with certainty, from the Grágás Code, that no other islands
were in this predicament than those now known to us, it
follows that the country in question was the Feröe Islands."

With trifling exceptions, the Editor freely accepts
all that Admiral Zahrtmann here says as true: but
true, not as a proof of the falsehood of the voyages
of the Zeni, but of exactly the contrary. It is quite
true that there was no such island as Frislanda, but,
from the names adduced by Admiral Zahrtmann himself as identical in Frislanda with those of the Færöe
Islands, it is equally obvious that the Færöe Islands
were represented by the Frislanda of the Zeno narrative and map. We must take things as we find
them, and while imperfect geography on a map of

the fourteenth or even of the sixteenth century is no
necessary proof of its inauthenticity, the occurrence of
names thereon which can be found in no other contemporary map or document, but which agree with
the known geography of to-day, is a very strong proof
indeed of its authenticity. But the Editor has still
further evidence to adduce in proof that the Feröe
Islands and Frislanda were identical. A description
is given in the text of a voyage made by Nicolò
Zeno to Frislanda to meet Zichmni on his return
from a victorious progress through the country. By
carefully following the text we shall with great
facility trace the route on a modern map, and realize
the several points visited, and thereby, *for the first
time*, remove the difficulties which have arisen from
conjectures as to what those places could be, as represented by the quaint and distorted spelling given to
them both in the ancient map and in the narrative.
It is one of those cases which show that apparent
trifles may prove of great moment. A more insignificant transaction than the passage which we are
about to trace on the map of the Færöe Islands could
scarcely be found in history, and yet it will go far to
settle a difficulty which has perplexed the minds of
some of the most distinguished literati of different
countries in Europe. We commence the route without even a shade of uncertainty. The words of the
narrative are, "They sailed to the westwards" (whence
is not said, but the following words render the omission of no importance), "and with little trouble gained
possession of Ledovo and Ilofe and other small islands

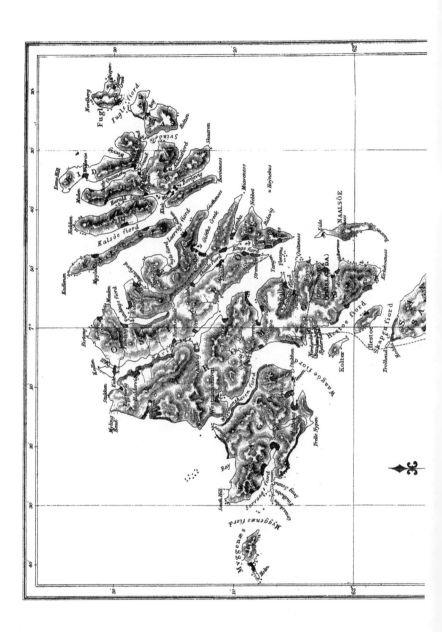

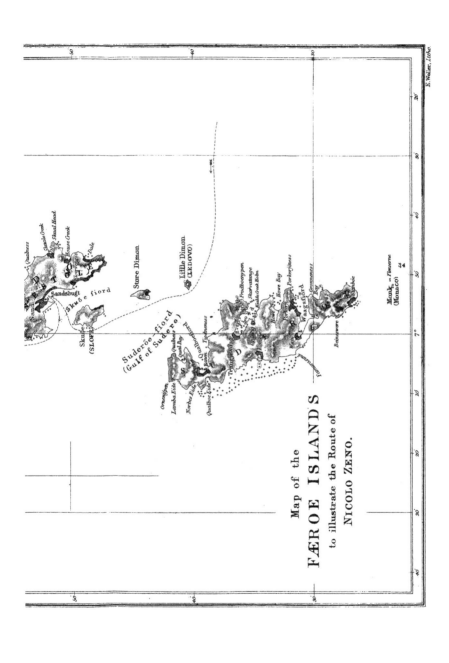

Map of the
FÆROE ISLANDS
to illustrate the Route of
NICOLO ZENO.

in a gulf called Sudero." The adjoining map will
show beyond all question that Sudero Gulf, or as
we call it Suderoe Fjord, lies between the islands of
Suderoe and Sandoe, and the islands described as
Ledovo and Ilofe, etc. must of necessity be Lille
Dimon, Store Dimon and Skuoe; and we have no
difficulty in understanding how the Venetian, Zeno,
hearing Lille Dimon uttered by a northerner, should
give to the sound which he heard the form of "Ledovo." A very good suggestion has been made by Bredsdorff in his article on the Zeno voyages in "Grönlands
Historiske Mindesmærker," that the " I " in Ilofe has
been mistakenly written by Nicolò Zeno, Junior, for
an "S" and thus we may see that Skuoe easily becomes,
when written down by the southerner, Slofe. The
text goes on to say that " in the Gulf of Suderoe in
the harbour of the country called Sanestol they captured some small barks laden with fish." The harbour of Sandsbugt in the island of Sandoe (Sanestol)
corresponds exactly with the position and description
of this unnamed harbour. The track thence is thus
described : " making their course still westwards,
they came to the other cape of the gulf," which cape
corresponds with the S. W. point of Sandoe as seen
in the modern map; "then turning again", i.e., round-
ing the cape, and consequently proceding northwards, " they fell in with certain islands and lands
which they brought into possession of Zichmni. This
sea was in a manner full of shoals and rocks." The
course being now northwards it is obvious that " the
sea" mentioned is that between Sandoe and Stromoe,

in which lie the small islets of Trothoved, Hestoe and Kolter. After passing these, " the captain determined to land at a place called Bondendon," and the track which the fleet was now taking leads straight into the harbour of Norderdahl, the name of which there is no difficulty in supposing transmuted by the Venetian into Bondendon. There they awaited Zichmni's arrival, and after the recital of what occurred when he arrived, the narrative states that "departing thence they went in triumphant manner towards Frislanda, the chief city of that island, on the south-east of it, lying inside a bay in which there is such great abundance of fish that many ships are laden therewith to supply Flanders, Britain, England, Scotland, Norway and Denmark, and by this trade they gather great wealth." Now knowing as we do the custom which obtained in the middle ages of giving to the capital of a country the name of the country itself, we can have little doubt that Frislanda was not the capital of the island only, but of the country to which that name was given; i.e., the whole Færoe group, and in it we accordingly recognise Thorshavn, the position of which on the island of Stromoe precisely tallies with that of Frislanda in the narrative. Nearly every man in Thorshavn is a fisherman, and it is a very curious and significant fact, that whereas we know that in all times a considerable amount of commerce was carried on with Iceland from the English ports of Bristol, Scarborough, etc., we have here an indication that the Færoe islands, which lay on the route from England to Iceland, were not

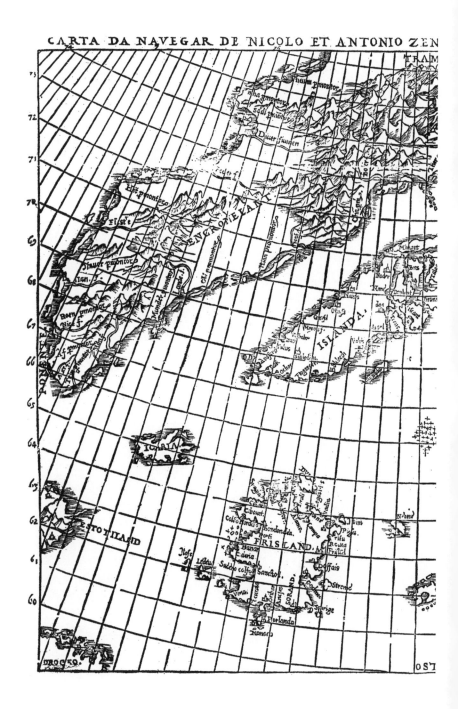

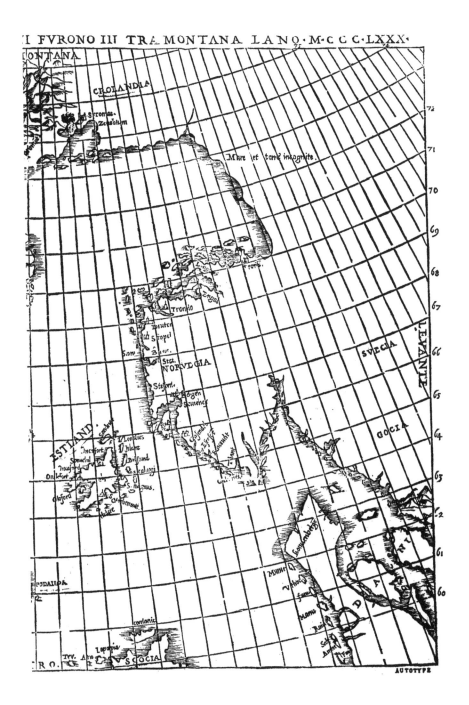

omitted from that intercourse at the close of the fourteenth century. Even if Admiral Zahrtmann had not already satisfactorily shown that Frislanda and the Færoe islands were identical, from the occurrence of such names as Andefjord, Stromoe, Monaco, etc., that fact would be conclusively established by the track which we have now been following; for, even although the reader should be disinclined to accept the suggested versions of the intermediate names, their individual and relative positions would nevertheless remain in harmony with the language of the text, while the entrance into the Gulf of Suderoe from the east at the commencement of it, and the position of Frislanda, the capital of the country, as the point of arrival at its close, correspond so exactly with the modern map as to leave no room for doubt. Now, when we turn from the Færoe islands of the modern map to the Frislanda of the Zeno map, of which the copy here given is a photographic *fac-simile*, we find indeed a single island of preposterous size, possibly because it had to receive the largest number of names; but it will also be seen that, in spite of the abnormal delineation of the island, the places indicated in our route-track occupy exactly corresponding positions thereon.

As to the word Frislanda, as Admiral Zahrtmann, himself a Dane, tells us that in old Danish these islands were called Færöisland, the transmutation is by no means difficult. Meanwhile, the inevitable fact remains that the Færoe group *was* represented by Nicolò Zeno, senior, in the four-

teenth century, by the word "Frislanda", and that
the process, whatever it may have been, must have
been easy, is proved by the fact that another
Italian, the illustrious Christopher Columbus, wrote
the same word down in exactly the same form in a
note preserved by his son Ferdinand in his father's
biography, where he says that, "in February 1477,
I sailed a hundred leagues beyond the island of
Tile, the southern part of which is not, as some
will have it, sixty-three, but seventy-three degrees
from the equinoctial line. It lies much more to the
west than the western meridian of Ptolemy. This
island is as large as England, and the English, especially those of Bristol, go there with their merchan-
dise. At the time that I was there the sea was not
frozen, but the tide runs so high as in some places
to rise and fall twenty-six fathoms. It is true that
the Tile mentioned by Ptolemy lies where he says it
does, and this is called by the moderns *Frislanda*."
   Now it is quite useless to spend time in discussing
the many geographical blunders embodied in this
short note. It is quite sufficient that Columbus gives
the word "Frislanda" in exactly the same form as
Zeno does, and even mentions it as a generally recognised name, and since it has already been demonstrated that Frislanda and the Færoe islands are
identical, even though in Columbus's blundering
note some sort of confusion has been made between
Iceland and the Færoe islands, his blunder does
not do away with that identity. Meanwhile, the
fact that he alludes to, of the men of Bristol carrying
their commerce into those seas (it is well known that

they traded largely with Iceland), presents to those
who approach the enquiry in the spirit of seeking
how the commutation of the word can possibly be
explained, instead of how it cannot be, a very reasonable explanation of the difficulty; but as it has been
objected by some, that Columbus may have picked
up the name from Zeno, it is necessary to state that
not only were the three men; Nicolò Zeno, senior,
of the close of the fourteenth century; Christopher
Columbus, of the close of the fifteenth century; and
Nicolò Zeno, junior, the editor of his ancestor's work
in the middle of the sixteenth century; perfectly independent of each other personally, but no one of
them had the means of knowing the name as coming
from any other of them. The Zeno story lay in the
Zeno palace, unknown to anybody and unvalued, until
found by Nicolò Zeno, junior, when he was a boy.
He was born in 1515, and Columbus died in 1506.
Nicolò Zeno, junior, published his ancestor's "Frislanda"
in 1558, long before anybody had heard of Columbus's allusion to the same name; for the statement
of the great navigator in which that name was mentioned was not given to the world till 1571, when
the Italian version of his son Ferdinand's biography
of his father was first printed.

But, in the above quoted arguments of Admiral
Zahrtmann, we have seen not only names adduced
which identify Frislanda with the Færoe islands;
but also similar evidence amply supplied from the
map—but, be it observed, not from the narrative—
of names establishing the identity of Estland with

the Shetland group. There is also very good reasoning, indeed, respecting the Orkneys and Caithness, the correctness of which must be fully acknowledged. But to these reasonings the editor would wish to add some corroborative observations of his own.

It will have been observed that Zichmni is styled Lord of Porlanda and Duke of Sorano. The language of the text is, " He [Zichmni] was a great Lord, and possessed some islands called Porlanda, near to Friesland, on the south"; and " besides the said small islands, he was Lord of the Duchy of Sorano, lying off the land and facing towards Scotland." If we look to the Zeno map, we find the name Porlanda placed against some islands between Suderoe [which means the southern island] and the Monk. Now, not only do no such islands exist; but, as Zichmni sails *from* Porland, his own domain, to attack Frisland, it is clear that the former was not *in* Frisland, but has been placed there by Nicolò Zeno, junior, under a misapprehension of the meaning of the statement of the text that "it lay near to Frisland on the south".

We have to look elsewhere, then, for Porlanda; and the narrative tells us to look southward from the Færoe islands and towards Scotland, where Sorano, another property of Zichmni, lay, and this points us direct to the Orkneys, which, it will be observed, are not laid down by their proper names, as we should have expected them to be on the Zeno map. We do, however, find " Podanda",[1] which is placed in

1 The cross-stroke of the " n" in this word is broken in the map,

the very direction indicated, and there can be little doubt that the "Podanda" of the map and the "Porlanda" of the text are identical, the "rl" of the one being easily mistakeable by Nicolò Zeno, junior, for the "d" of the other. And now we shall see how this fits in with other facts. It is to the learned Johann Reinhold Forster that we are indebted for the valuable suggestion that Zichmni is the Venetian Zeno's rendering for Sinclair. It was in 1379 that Henry Sinclair of Roslyn was invested by Hacon VI, King of Norway, with the earldom of the Orkneys and Caithness. The declaration of Sinclair's fealty to the King is given entire by Torfæus in his "History of the Orkneys", p. 174. It will now be seen how Zichmni, Lord of Porlanda, is Sinclair, Lord of the Orkneys. But why Porlanda for Orkneys? In the absence of certainty, the editor ventures on a suggestion. Throughout the narrative this chieftain is never mentioned by his title, but always by his surname. When once, therefore, Zeno had made a note of the territorial possessions of this chief as they might chance to be communicated to him, there would arise nothing in daily intercourse to correct such memorandum if it were either inaccurate or inadequate. We will suppose, therefore, Zeno cruising in the Pentland Frith, which lies betwixt Sinclair's lordships of Orkney and Caithness, and he is informed by the sailors that he is now in the midst of the domains of his lordship. He there-

and looks like "li", and was so read by Admiral Zahrtmann; but it is really "n".

upon takes note from their lips of the names of those
domains as they lie respectively on the north and
on the south.   On the north he would have Pentland, which by misspelling, misreading from the old
writing, or by Venetian transmutation, becomes,
finally, Podanda or Porlanda ; we have the island
of Swona in the Pentland Frith (in exactly the position indicated by the text : " fra terra posta della
banda verso Scotia"), which becomes written down
in the text Sorano, and on the south we have Con-
tanes, which is beyond all question Caithness, for it is
found under that form in several other documents.
It is necessary to dwell on the exact correspondence
of Swona with the position of the Sorano of the text,
in order to establish its identity in spite of the
ridiculous epithet of "Duchea" which is attached
thereto.   Whether the use of the word originated in
ignorance, or bombast,[1] or both, we must remember
that the portion of the text in which it occurs was a
compilation by Nicolò Zeno, junior, from the letters of his ancestral namesake ; that the latter was
ignorant of the language of the north, and would
pick up his information with difficulty ; and that
epistolary correspondence can scarcely be expected to
embody the severe accuracy of history.   The acceptance by many commentators of this most unquestionable blunder of placing Porlanda in the Færoe Islands has led only to confusion ; whereas under this

[1] The grandiloquence which could enlarge a rocky islet into a
Duchy is a characteristic of the narrative which will be treated of
more specially presently.

new suggestion a variety of unquestionable facts are brought into harmonious combination. But now that we have seen that the Zeno map possesses the merit of containing a variety of names of places in the Færoe group, which we might hope in vain to find in any other map, even of the comparatively late period (1558), when it was engraved and published,— places recognisable by the light of modern geography. —let us turn and see what absurd blunders it exhibits in the misplacement of localities through the want of that light, by Nicolò Zeno, junior, the very man to whom we are indebted for the document itself. It may be asked on what ground these blunders are attributed to him. The answer is very simple. They are all of the most preposterous character, unlike anything else on the map. They consist of *those names and those only which occur in the narrative,* and as the bearings in the narrative agree with modern geography, it follows, beyond all doubt, that the blunders have arisen from the misreading of it. The narrative gives an account of a second victorious campaign, this time directed against Estland, which it describes as lying upon the coast between Frisland and Norway, and which unmistakeably, therefore, is Shetland. "Here they did much damage, but hearing that a fleet of the King of Norway's was coming to oppose them, they departed, but with such a gale of wind that they lost several of their vessels, and the rest were driven on a large but uninhabited island, called Grislanda, lying to the south." Nicolò Zeno, junior, misreading Esland for Iceland, places

xxiv   INTRODUCTION.

Grislanda off the south coast of that island, and in
pursuance of the same mistake, endows Iceland with
a cluster of seven islands on its eastern coast, which
will presently be seen to belong to Shetland. Now
south of Shetland lie the Orkneys, the Mainland of
which is called Hross-ey or Gross-ey, and just as
the Færoe Islands or Færoisland became to Italian
ears Frislanda, so would Gross-ey or Gross Island
become Grislanda, and that this, whatever the process
of derivation may be, is really correct we shall immediately have proof. News came that the enemy's fleet
had been entirely wrecked in the said storm, and
Zichmni seeing that the Shetlands (already described
as lying between the Færoes and Norway, and called
in the Italian "le Islande" in the plural, consequently
not Iceland, but evidently "the Shetlands") *lay not
far off to the northward* (exactly their position with
respect to the Orkneys), resumed his purpose.

The first place that he approached was called
Islanda, and just as we have seen that the word
"Frislanda" was used for the capital of Frislanda or
the Færoe Islands, so we must infer that "Islanda"
is here the capital of the "Islande" or Shetland
Islands, wherever that may have been. Lerwick
did not then exist. He found it so well protected,
that he removed his attack to the other islands in
those channels, called the Shetlands, seven in number : Talas (Yelli), Broas (East and West Barras),
Iscant (Unst), Trans (St. Ronan's Isle), Mimant
(Mainland), Dambere (Hamna), and Bres (Bressay).
He took them all, and built a fort in Bres, where he

left Messire Nicolò with some vessels and men and
stores, and he himself returned to Frisland. Now,
there is no doubt that "Islanda" was a proper form
for Iceland, and therefore eminently calculated to
mislead Nicolò Zeno, junior, but it is hoped that from
the position of the islands in question, between the
Færoe Islands and Norway, from their description as
lying "in those channels", from the correspondence
of the individual names with the islands, and the
plural generic name "le Islande" for the group, no
doubt will be left on the reader's mind as to the
"Islande" being the Shetland Islands and not Iceland,
and that Grislanda occupies the position of Gross-ey
in the Orkneys, the wild coast of which would give
it the aspect of being uninhabited to any one
driven on it in a storm. Yet it will have been
seen that while the narrative is consistent with itself and with modern geography, the map places
Grislanda to the south of Iceland, and the islands
which have been identified with Shetland are engrafted on the east coast of Iceland. In this fact
we have a proof that Nicolò Zeno, junior, the re-
storer of the map, is the cause of all the perplexity.
But while this is a proof of his ignorance of the
geography, it is the greatest proof that could be
desired that he could not possibly have been the
ingenious concocter of a narrative, the demonstrable
truth of which, when checked by modern geography,
he could thus ignorantly distort upon the face of a
map.

Ignorance of the geography of the north in the

*

middle of the sixteenth century cannot be looked upon as a reproach to him, but it had its consequences, and the editor dwells upon them because he claims the argument as a demonstration, now advanced for the first time, of the authenticity and truth of the original documents.

He ventures to maintain that this proof is so conclusive that it could not be invalidated, even if we were unable to find a solution of some of the puzzles which the narrative and map present to us. Such, however, is happily not the case. We shall find that all of them can be met with explanations, based not on mere fancy or opinion, but on solid and substantial arguments and facts ; and the result is, that when we have once been able to detach that which is erroneous from that which is correct, we find that those portions of the ancient story which have not been marred by misreading, exaggeration, or unintelligent interference, are, with one exception, which will be spoken of hereafter, in harmony with the knowledge which we possess in the present day.

But we must not yet quit this subject of the attack upon Shetland, which the narrative would lead us to understand involved a conflict with the King of Norway.   On this point, Zahrtmann says :

"As to the war asserted to have been waged between Zichmni and the King of Norway, this assertion is the less entitled to belief, from the circumstance that there was no king in Norway, that country being at that period under the government of Queen Margaret.   Forster's opinion, that Zichmni might have been Henry Sinclair, Earl of the Orkneys, is altogether destitute of foundation ; as that

lord, on whom the said earldom was bestowed in 1380
[say rather 1379] by King Haagan, both in 1388 and 1389
—as a Norwegian councillor of state—signed the act by
which Eric of Pomerania was acknowledged true heir of the
realm, and therefore at that time could not have been in
rebellion against the crown. Neither is there any reason
for supposing that his earldom, which comprehended Shetland, was in the meantime attacked and completely ravaged,
and yet the Danish history make no allusion to any such
circumstance ; more especially when we again, in 1397, find
that Jonas, Bishop of the Orkneys, signed in Calmar the
coronation act of Eric of Pomerania, which shows that the
connection between the islands and the mother country
had continued without interruption."

This criticism of Admiral Zahrtmann's is perfectly
just and reasonable from his point of view, a point
of view most certainly, *primâ facie*, sanctioned by
the language of the text. But is there no possibility
that that language itself may not be perfectly correct ? We have already seen how the editorial in-
tervention of Nicolò Zeno, junior, introduced inac-
curacies into the map, which have been a perplexity
and a trap to commentators ever since. Now, no
one can read the text without perceiving that while
he has fortunately given us entire pieces of original
matter, he has himself supplied the cement which
binds the whole together.

We have also seen by the example of the map,
that he was capable of incorporating into his publication his own views of the facts related in the documents which he had before him ; and yet there is
no legitimate reason to doubt that this was done conscientiously. Now, as we shall presently see, the

narrative, as we have received it from him, exhibits beyond all contradiction a quality excessively misleading to the critic who takes each word *au pied de la lettre,* and that quality is hyperbole: yet no one it may be hoped, who is acquainted with the genius of the southern mind, would condemn a tendency to a certain amount of hyperbole, especially in the record of the deeds of an ancestor, as involving any conscious want of integrity. At the same time, it is even quite possible that some or all of the inflation of the language may have existed in the original letter. Of this we have no means of judging. Nicolò Zeno, junior, we do know; Nicolò Zeno, senior, we do not, in regard of the sophistication, however blameless, of the matter which has reached our hands. But that hyperbole has been indulged in by the early Nicolò, or the later, or both, may be judged from the following sentence. When Nicolò's fleet reached Bondendon (Norderdahl),

"They heard to their great satisfaction that Zichmni had fought a great battle, and put to flight the army of the enemy; in consequence of which victory, ambassadors were sent from all parts of the island to yield the country up into his hands, taking down their ensigns in every town and village."

It would be difficult to find in all literature a more striking example of grandiloquence and bombast in the description of so petty an occurrence. And yet it would be as unwise to condemn the reality of the scene, on account of the vividness of the colouring, as it would be to utter a sweeping condemnation of the hospitality of a Spaniard, be-

cause he places his house and all that he possesses at our disposal. Nevertheless, under the
rigid exactness of criticism, this hyperbole has ex-
posed the document to the gravest suspicions, simply because all hyperbole is a deviation from strict
truth. Not only is the scantiness of towns and villages and population in the Færoe Islands utterly at
variance with the strict letter of the above description; but the known gentleness of the people would
lead, and to the editor's own knowledge has led, to
a denial of the truth of the story of the attack on
Zeno, when first wrecked on their shores. The editor
objects to this denial on the grounds already advanced, and submits that as we have already had unanswerable proof of the general authenticity of the
story, we must accept the exaggerations as merely
the husk which surrounds a real and genuine kernel.
All deviation from right is wrong, though from habit
it may not be so reputed. In France good men,
gentle ladies, and innocent children are in the con-
stant habit of breaking the third commandment, and
yet it may be doubted if any one could be found so unreasonable as to charge such persons with the offence
of wilful blasphemy. Although, however, we may
not suppose that, through that habit, the third commandment is abrogated, we may hope that habit,
combined with the absence of a wrong intention, may
prove the strongest excuse for those whom, according to the strict letter of the law, the Almighty has
declared that He will not hold guiltless. The lesson
is, that if we would not fail in the search after truth,

we must recognise realities which bear the characteristic of elasticity, as well as those which have to be
measured with mathematical precision. And so it is
with hyperbole, but between the two cases there is this
difference. An offence against the third commandment is an offence against the Almighty, but there
it stops. In that amount of deviation from truth
which we call hyperbole, man's judgment is concerned, and it becomes eminently desirable that there
should be no mistake about the correctness of the
facts in the statement of which exaggeration is re-
sorted to ; for it is obvious that then the statement
will be most dangerously misleading. Now it must
be acknowledged that the elder Nicolò Zeno ran a
great risk of imperfectly apprehending facts in the
simple circumstance of his ignorance of the language of those amongst whom he moved. Whatever may have been the character of Sinclair's so-
called triumphant expedition in the Færoe Islands,
it appears pretty certain that there has been great
misapprehension on the part of Nicolò Zeno, senior,
as to the motives of Sinclair's movements in the
Shetland islands, or else there have been both misreading and exaggeration on the part of Nicolò Zeno,
junior, in dressing up the story.

Exaggeration is patent enough in the statements
that "hearing that the King of Norway was coming
against them with a great fleet to draw them off
from this attack, they departed under a terrible gale
of wind," and that "the King of Norway's fleet being
caught in the same storm, was utterly wrecked."

We can scarcely suppose the king to have acted in such a movement in person, or that his whole fleet was wrecked, and yet so notable an event be unrecorded in history. Exaggeration, however, is not the only difficulty in the way of our comprehending this attack on the Shetland Islands. Admiral Zahrtmann truly states that Sinclair's "earldom comprehended Shetland." Sir William Douglas tells us in his "Peerage of Scotland," p. 337, that the earldom had come into the family by the marriage of Henry Sinclair's father, Sir William Sinclair of Roslyn, with Isabelle, one of the daughters and co-heiress of Malise, Earl of Strathern, Caithness, and Orkney. The last Scandinavian Yarl was Magnus, the father of Malise's first wife. Among the charters of Robert III, King of Scotland, is one confirming a charter dated the 23rd of April, 1391, by Henry de Sancto Claro, Earl of Orkney and Lord of Roslyn, to David de Sancto Claro his brother, of the lands of Newburgh and Auchdale in Aberdeenshire, "pro suo homagio et bono servitio nobis impenso, et pro toto tempore vitæ suæ impendendo, ac etiam pro suo jure et clameo aliquali in partibus Orcadiæ seu Schetlandiæ sibi ratione Isabellæ de Sancto Claro, matris suæ, aliquo modo contingente."

By this we see that Shetland was included in the earldom, and we also see the ambiguous position in which Henry Sinclair stood with reference to the two sovereigns of Norway and Scotland.

It was from the King of Norway that Henry Sinclair had received in 1379 the recognition of his claim to the Earldom of Orkney, but his investiture was burdened with severe conditions. He was bound to serve the King with a hundred well-armed men whenever required, upon a notice of three months; to defend the Orkneys and Shetland against any invasion, not only with the native force, but with the whole power of his house; to assist the king when he attacked any foreign state; not to build any castles or ports in the islands without the royal consent, and to assist the king against the Bishop of Orkney, who belonged virtually to the Scottish Church, with other clauses which need not here be enumerated.

We have in the "Orcades" of Torfæus, pp. 174-7, Sinclair's own Declaration of Fealty to the King of Norway, in which all these pledges on his part are fully detailed. If therefore we took the Zeno narrative *au pied de la lettre* as regards this attack upon Shetland, and understood it as a real conflict with the King of Norway, we should find ourselves in a dilemma from which it would be next to impossible to escape, for by such a transaction the earldom would be forfeited.

Now there is very strong reason for suspecting that, in the present case, exaggeration, employed only for the glorification of the occasion, has, from a foreigner's liability to misapprehend the true state of the case, led to the introduction of a false element into the story. Only let it be assumed that the same bombastic style of description which introduced armies and ambassadors and taking down of ensigns

in every town and village of the poor and scantily
peopled island of Stromoe, has with equal accuracy,
in the present case, brought the King of Norway
with a large fleet upon the scene of action, and our
difficulty will disappear. The editor has an historical
incident to adduce which will not only present a reasonable explanation of the mistake into which, under this
assumption, Zeno would have fallen as to the political
nature of the conflict, but it tallies both in time[1] and
place with the Zeno story, and involves no infringe-
ment of Sinclair's fealty to the King of Norway. In
Sinclair's Declaration of Fealty (Torfæus, "Orcades,"
p. 176) occurs the following passage, "We also promise
that, since we have been already promoted by our
Lord the King himself to the earldom and lordship
aforesaid, our cousin Malise Sperre must cease from
his claim and altogether lay aside his very claim itself,
if it is decided that he has any, to the said lands and
islands, so that our Lord the King, his heirs and
successors, shall endure no vexation or annoyance
from him or from his heirs."[2] Then, at page 178 of
Torfæus occurs the following entry : Anno MCCCXCI,
Comes Orcadensis occidit Mallisium Sparrium in

---

[1] The question of date will be fully dealt with a few pages
further on.

[2] Item promittimus quia ad comitatum, et ad dominium sæpe
fatum, per ipsum Dominum nostrum Regem sumus jam promoti,
quod consanguineus noster Malisius Sperre cessare debet a jure
suo, et ipsum jus suum omnino dimittere, si quod ad ipsas terras
et insulas habere dignoscitur, ita quod Dominus noster Rex, hære-
des sui vel successores, nullam ab eo, aut ab ejus hæredibus vexa-
tionem vel molestiam sustinebunt.

Hialtlandia cum septem aliis. Juvenis autem quidam cum sex aliis, navem sex *(sic)* scalmorum nactus in Norvegiam fugâ evasit. "In the year 1391, the Earl of Orkney slew Malise Sperre in Shetland with seven others. A certain youth, however, with six others, procured a vessel at Scalloway and escaped to Norway." We have seen how the earldom passed by marriage from the old Scandinavian yarls into the house of Sinclair, and the name of Sinclair's cousin Malise Sperre is suggestive that he was of the Norse side of the family, and that in that capacity he put in the rival claim to the inheritance, of which Sinclair himself speaks. Torfæus does not inform us of the immediate cause of the conflict in which Sperre was slain by Sinclair in Shetland, but there can be little doubt that that cause was the disputed lordship of Shetland, and that Sinclair, in the incident recorded by Zeno, was taking possession *de facto* of that which he already possessed *de jure*, while his contests with his Norse rival would easily bear to Zeno's intelligence the aspect of a conflict with Norway. It must be borne in mind that the authenticity of the Zeno document being now fundamentally established, we are not called upon to do more than show the *possibility* of any of the facts related, but in the incident just recited it must be allowed that we have a case not of possibility only, but of high probability.

It can scarcely be doubted that one of the leading causes of the Zeno puzzle having remained unsolved till now, has been the tendency to cope with the outlying difficulties instead of first directing atten-

tion to the proof of the authenticity of the document.
That such a tendency does exist may be seen by the
following suggestion made to the editor in the most
friendly manner by a learned and honoured corre-
spondent, who was a firm believer in the ungenuineness
of the Zeno story. "It is quite right", he says, "that
such an author ought to be studied carefully, and
every thing that can possibly establish the veracity
of his statements ought to be adduced and taken
into account; but not, I think, till all objections have
been satisfactorily reasoned away."

If such a plan had been persistently adhered to,
the Zeno mystery would, in all probability, have
remained a mystery till the crack of doom. It is by
the introduction of every attainable ray of light that
truth is discovered, and with the gradual discovery
of truth, objections, which are so often, as in this
case, the children of misapprehension, however ex-
cusable, either become explained or fall into their
right place. The genuineness of the work lies at the
root of the whole question. Indeed, the authenticity
of the document is so preponderating an element in
the case, that, when once it is well established, the
minor objections might be fairly left to shake themselves into their places as best they could. It is not,
however, intended so to leave them, but the remark
is introduced here specially in application to the present position of the argument. If the editor had undertaken to cope with Admiral Zahrtmann's reasonings
on his second proposition without the demonstrations
which have been now arrived at, he could have done

so only with extreme difficulty and at great length, whereas now he hopes that his readers will themselves perceive that these difficulties vanish into air. We now come to Admiral Zahrtmann's second proposition, which is couched in the following terms : "That the said chart has been compiled from hearsay informa- tion, and not by any seaman who had himself navi- gated in those seas for several years." The last clause of this proposition, of course, must be understood to mean, "was not laid down from actual survey." Quite true. Now, seeing that it was compiled from hearsay information ; that it supplies us with names of places in the Shetland group, and in the Færoe islands, etc., remarkably in advance of what is laid down on any map, even of the comparatively late period of Nicolò Zeno, junior's, publication in 1558 ; what could we ask for more in harmony with the statement of the latter in that publication, viz. : "Of these north parts I have thought good to draw a copy of the sailing chart, which I find that I still have amongst our family antiquities, and although it is rotten with age, I have succeeded with it tolerably well"?

When Admiral Zahrtmann recognises that "the old forms of Foer-eyar and Orkn-eyar, which are not found on the map, are difficult to Italianise or even to be at all caught or retained by any Italian ear, and that names are transposed in the spirit of the Italian language", and when he draws the just in- ference that these names were not copied from any other chart, but laid down from verbal depositions, how can that inference be other than confirmative of the fact that the map "rotten with age" contained these names as they were received from northern tongues by the Zeno of the fourteenth century, and written down by him or them after being distilled through the alembic of a southern mind ? If this map had been a compilation of Nicolò Zeno, junior, from any other chart or charts, this phenomenon would not have been exhibited, but the names would have been copied from the northern sources in their native northern form. But it must never be forgotten that the old chart *was* " rotten with age", that Nicolò Zeno, junior, had " drawn a copy of it", and, as he flattered himself, "had succeeded with it tolerably well." It is clear that in this attempt, having a desire to remedy the damages of the old chart and to make his copy as complete as possible, he had recourse to the narrative for guidance; but, unhappily, not possessing maps at that early period which could set him right when he misread the narrative, his very laudable effort resulted in the most deplorable confusion, and has, in fact, been the cause of very nearly all the doubts and discussions and disbelief to which this ill-starred document has given rise. Hence, we have on the face of the same map two opposite realities : good geography, in advance even of the period at which it was published, side by side with the most preposterous blunders. But the explanation is manifest, the good was of the fourteenth century, gathered by the ear on the spot, the bad was of the sixteenth century, misapprehended from the ancient narrative.

We now come to Admiral Zahrtmann's arguments
on his second proposition : " That the said chart has
been compiled from hearsay information, and not by
any seaman who had himself navigated in those seas
for several years."

" As to the second point", he says : " it is in the first
place hardly credible, that a seaman acquainted with the
navigation of the Northern Seas should have assigned so in-
correct a relative position to the different places. For example, that Shetland (from which may be seen the Orkneys,
lying close under the coast of Scotland) should be represented as situated near Norway, far distant from Scotland,
and without any intermediate islands. The same fault, however, is found, to a greater or less degree, in all the maps
published in the sixteenth century, which shows that the
chart of the Zeni is, in this respect, a copy. We are perfectly
acquainted from the Landnama-Book with every particular
of Iceland in the thirteenth century, and we know that it
was then just the same as now ; how, then, is it possible
that a seaman, who had resided there for so long a time,
should represent it like an archipelago of several considerable
islands ? How could he have remained ignorant of the
native names of the places, particularly of the harbours, and
have only learned the Latin names of the island and its two
dioceses ? How could he give it a shape which, though it
is called by Malte-Brun, in his ' Précis de la Géographie uni-
verselle', ' bonne à l'exception de la partie Nord Ouest', in
truth resembles any other place as much as Iceland ? How
could he lay down to the north-east of Iceland a continent
upon which he pretends to have been, when we know that
in that direction there exists no continent, but only the
island of Jan Mayen ? And finally, how could he have been
in the Feröe islands, and yet represent them as one large
island surrounded by some smaller ones ? The whole chart
bears the most palpable marks of having been compiled by a
person who had never been at the places themselves, and

who knew nothing of either the language or the history of
the North; for the Sagas and Sailing Directions prove,
that in those days the inhabitants of the North had much
juster ideas of the relative position of places, and that they
knew, for example, that a line drawn from Bergen, between
Shetland and the Feroe Islands, would pass about sixty
geographical miles to the southward of Iceland. The chart
is dated 1380, an epoch at which Zurla has proved that both
Nicolò and Antonio Zeno were in Italy; which shows that
they had not drawn the chart at the places themselves,—for
as to the possibility of their having ante-dated it, it is to be
presumed that in those days there was as little inducement as
there is now for the framer of a chart to publish it as older than
it really was. Finally, the comparative correctness of the delineation of Denmark and Norway is the best proof that the
chart was not drawn in 1380, but about the middle of the sixteenth century. Zurla himself mentions that in the Isolario
of Benedetto Bordone, published at Venice in 1534, Norway
and Greenland are very erroneously laid down,—a topic to
which we shall have to return hereafter. The exiled Archbishop of Upsala, Olaus Magnus Gothus, published at Venice,
in 1539, a map of the three Scandinavian kingdoms, which
I have not seen, as it appears doubtful whether any copy of
it remains in existence; but undoubtedly this map, and those
published at Antwerp, particularly those of Ortelius, were
the first that gave a tolerably correct representation of these
countries, an accurate knowledge of which it was impossible
for the Zeni to have procured at any of the places visited
by them,—viz., Frisland, Estland, Iceland, and Greenland."

With what has been already written present to
his mind, the reader will be able, it is hoped, to see
how, with the exception of the date which will be
dealt with presently, answers can be given to the
objections here brought against the authenticity of
the map. He will be able to see, what Admiral

Zahrtmann did not see, that Iceland is, in truth, not brought into question at all in the part of the narrative under review, but that Nicolò Zeno, junior, through misreading the name, mistook Shetland for Iceland and added to the latter the names belonging to the former. We cannot answer for how much of the map may be due to his handiwork, but of this we may be sure, that information therein, which was in advance of the knowledge of his day, and coincident with the knowledge of our own, was derived from the early visit to the spot, while deviations from correctness, even though not his own, are no proof of inauthenticity in a map of the fourteenth century.

The remainder of Admiral Zahrtmann's facts, comments and insinuations, are not so categorically arranged, but the editor has analysed them all, and for the sake of clearness has grouped them in the order in which they bear upon the narrative and its publication.

"It cannot be denied", says Zahrtmann, "that the story has been composed with great ingenuity, but still it contains contradictions. We may ask, for example, how was Nicolò Zeno informed that Antonio spent fourteen years in Frisland, when no mention is made of this either in the last complete letter, or in that fragment which was the last discovered, and in which he says he has only made some alterations in the style and the obsolete expressions, but not in substance? If it was from the dates of the letters, he certainly could not mistake ten years in fixing the epoch when the voyages were performed. Neither is it to be believed that in a family like that of the Zeni, where, not less than three, viz., Jacopo, Nicolò, and Pietro, each in his century, published descriptions of the exploits of their ancestors, the

children should have been suffered to destroy the family
archives, or that records similar to Antonio's description of
the North should have been left unnoticed and unpublished
for more than a century—at a period, too, when Columbus's
transcendent discovery attracted universal attention to the
West. That the family could not have been ignorant of
their contents is proved by the circumstance of Nicolò
knowing what he had destroyed, which, as he himself was a
child at the time, he could only have learned at a later
period from his parents. Allowing, however, that Nicolò,
when a child, did really destroy the work of his own direct
ancestor, Antonio, it still remains to be explained how he
had it in his power to destroy several of the letters, they
being all addressed to Carlo, the most respected of the brothers, who survived all the rest, and whose direct descendants
did not become extinct till a whole century later : viz., in
1653. Even supposing that the whole of the family archives
were deposited with the senior branch, the chance of their
falling into the younger Nicolò's hands remains as unlikely
as ever, inasmuch as he was descended from Antonio, the
second son, whose elder brother's lineage was not extinct
before the year 1756."

The reply to all which is, that whatever part of
American soil may be referred to in the Zeno narrative, it was in no sense connected by Nicolò Zeno's
ancestors with the idea of a trans-atlantic world, for it
had been only regarded as a continuation of Europe.
We could ask no better proof that his parents did
not attach this extreme value to these papers than
the fact that they did not secure them from being
torn up by a child, and it is clear that neither then
nor afterwards could they communicate to him what
they had no idea of themselves. Comparatively unimportant, however, as these papers would therefore, in

this sense, be to them, it is most easy of belief, and most natural, that Nicolò's father or grandfather should have received from a cousin, one of Carlo's descendants, the letters addressed to Carlo, simply as describing the exploits, whatever their value, of his own direct ancestor. When, however, Nicolò Zeno approached manhood, North America began to be known, and hence the recognition by him of the value of the papers which had lain hitherto neglected in the palace. That family papers, more or less important, may fall into a child's hands and be destroyed or damaged, is too certain to need of argument; and the chances and changes of this mortal life have not, we may suppose, been sent to all God's creatures to the single exclusion of the Zeno family.

Admiral Zahrtmann raises a great question as to which of three Nicolò Zenos mentioned in the Venetian Annals at the close of the fourteenth century was hero of the voyages. There need be no question at all on the subject. Nicolò Zeno, junior, tells us in his genealogy at the beginning of·the narrative that his own direct ancestor Antonio, and Nicolò the Cavalier, the heroes of the voyages, were brothers of the famous Carlo, who, in 1382, saved the Republic, and thereby so much increased the reputation of the family. This Nicolò the Cavalier, was, for distinction's sake, called "quondam Ser Dracone", and in Muratori's *Rerum Italicarum Scriptores*, tome 22, p. 779, we find him mentioned by this same designation as one of the three syndics who were elected on the 14th December, 1388, to take possession of the city of Treviso. After this date, however, no mention of him occurs in the Venetian Annals, and as we are told in the Zeno narrative that he died while out in the north, a victim to the climate, Cardinal Zurla very justly says that this silence respecting him in the Annals is in conformity with the fact that he was away from his country and engaged in the voyages as represented. We have, therefore, no room left for doubt as to his identity. But, this being so, it is evident that the date of 1380, given both in the text and on the map, must be erroneous, and we shall presently see from other evidence that such in very truth is the case, and that the date has really to be placed ten years later. In dealing with this discrepancy of ten years in fixing the epoch when the voyages were performed, Admiral Zahrtmann's indictment against Nicolò Zeno, junior, takes the following shape.

"According to Cardinal Zurla," he says, "Nicolò cannot have left Venice till 1390, and it is certain that in 1406 Antonio was already dead. Of that interval Antonio is said to have spent fourteen years in Frisland. There remain, therefore, scarcely two years for Nicolò to have completed his perilous voyage, to have been wrecked, to have made his first brilliant campaign, ending in the conquest of Frisland, and to have reported it to Antonio (whom he actually induced to perform the voyage from Venice), and finally to have died there, and all within the interval of two years. Even now-a-days this would scarcely be possible."

The editor cannot but express his amazement at such an assertion. Suffering shipwreck is usually not a lengthy process. The brilliant campaign in Frisland,

which we have followed in the preceding pages, must
have been a very lazy operation if it occupied a week;
so that if we deduct these events from two years,
there will be left "ample space and verge enough"
for the two voyages out and the transmission of a
letter between, and a great deal of time to spare into
the bargain. To call the crowding of these events
into two years an impossibility is simply absurd. On
the strength, however, of such assumed impossibility
Admiral Zahrtmann proceeds to say :

"Yet it is on the authority of Antonio's letters, which
Nicolò Zeno, junior, pretends to have had in his possession,
that he has written this narrative. From the same letters
he must have drawn his dates, and a solitary error in this
respect could easily have been detected, as there were several
letters. Now, as the dates of these letters correspond exactly
with the time at which Zurla has clearly proved that the
brothers were in Italy, it follows that the letters from Frisland were either fabrications or that they never existed."

The date of 1380, it is true, stands in Roman numerals on the Zeno map, and is written out in full in
the narrative. But facts are stubborn things, and if we
conscientiously and industriously resort to them instead of to preconceived conclusions, we shall generally arrive pretty near the truth at last. Admiral
Zahrtmann elsewhere shows his perfect knowledge
of a remarkable fact, which, if he had been as
anxious to find where Zeno was right, as where he
might be made out to be wrong, would have rectified
the above error of 1380 and neutralised all the
arguments that he founds upon it.

A relative of the family, named Marco Barbaro, wrote, in 1536, a copious work, entitled " Discendenze Patrizie", on Venetian noble families, and in the genealogical table of the Zeno family makes the following entry under the name of Antonio Zeno. " Scrisse con il fratello Nicolò Kav. li viaggi dell' Isole sotto il polo artico, e di quei scoprimente del 1390, e che per ordine di Zicno, Re di Frislanda, si portò nel continente d'Estotilanda nell' America setten-trionale, e che si fermò 14 anni in Frislanda, cioè 4 con suo fratello Nicolò e 10 solo." " He wrote with his brother, Nicolò the Cavalier, the voyages of the islands under the Arctic Pole, and of those discoveries of 1390, and that by order of Zicno, King of Frisland, he went to the continent of Estotilànd in North America. He dwelt fourteen years in Frisland, four with his brother Nicolò, and ten alone." Cardinal Zurla first mentioned this fact, and the editor has verified it, by procuring an extract of the entry from Venice, through the kindness of his distinguished friend Mr. Rawdon Brown. Admiral Zahrtmann adverts to it, solely to make the following insinuation :

" It must be observed," says he, " that this work is a manuscript, and that it is therefore impossible to decide when or by whom any article in it was written, and as the families of Zeno and Barbaro were related to each other and on most friendly terms, Nicolò Zeno, who was the firstborn of the family, might very well have been intrusted with the drawing up of the family genealogy"—

implying thereby that little trust was to be placed in a statement possibly drawn up by one whom he,

Admiral Zahrtmann, had mentally condemned as an impostor. But here he overshot the mark. There is little doubt that Barbaro did derive this statement from Nicolò Zeno, who had so nearly, but not quite, destroyed when a boy, the old papers on which it was based. But in drawing up the said statement Nicolò Zeno showed that he was cognisant in 1536, two-and-twenty years before the Zeno narrative and map were printed, of that true date of 1390, which coincided exactly with the evidence of the annals of his country.

If both the dates 1380 and 1390 emanated from him, one was clearly a mistake, and as we can have no doubt which was the erroneous one, we have in the error itself, whether made through carelessness in either one or both cases by Nicolò, or by the printer, or by the engraver, a proof that Nicolò was not at least the subtle and ingenious concocter of falsehoods that Admiral Zahrtmann would represent him to be. Nicolò Zeno held the high position of Member of the Council of Ten of the Republic, and had all his country's annals at his command. As the historian of his family, he had those annals intimately within his own cognisance. Did it never, therefore, strike Admiral Zahrtmann, that if Zeno had been the cunning and laborious impostor he would make him to be, there was nothing he would more carefully have avoided, or could have avoided with greater ease, than the lapsus of giving an enemy the opportunity of proving an *alibi* against his ancestors in the matter in question ? The conclusion is evident

therefore that 1380 was an error, and when it is
considered that this date is written above the map
in Roman numerals, thus : MCCCLXXX, it will be seen
how easily that easiest of all delinquencies either of
the author, the editor, or the engraver ; viz,—the
dropping of a final x, may have occurred. The short
sentence in the narrative " this was in one thousand
three hundred and eighty," most certainly occurs in a
a part written by Nicolò Zeno, junior, and the legend
at the top of the map is manifestly by him also, so that
there is a common origin for both. How the blunder
may have occurred however, is all conjecture, but
enough has been said to prove that *it was* a blunder,
and it may well be asked whether, on the strength of
such an accident, a nobleman of high and ancient lineage, the members of whose family had many of them
so eminently distinguished themselves in the history
of their country as to stand in no need of falsehoods
to add to their glory, himself a Member of the Council
of Ten, is to be branded as a concocter of falsehoods ?

That there is reason in the editor's suggestion
about the possible dropping of an " x" in the date
is shown by a remarkable fact.   The great Antwerp
geographer Ortelius, in recording this very narrative,
copied the Roman numerals as they stand at the top
of the map, making 1380, yet when our Hakluyt
produced the same story on the authority of Ortelius,
he gave the date of 1390, thus proving by a con-
verse blunder how easily this kind of error may
occur.

But now that we have 1390 for Nicolò Zeno's

arrival in the Færoes, and 1391 for the exploits in
the Shetland islands (see ante, page xxxiv), in which
Antonio was present, there are but three transactions to be accounted for in the interval, the attack
on the Færoes, the transmission of Nicolò's invitation,
and Antonio's voyage out, and to say that a year
and a half, and possibly more, was not sufficient for
all this, would be an absurdity. With these dates
also before us, we see that ample time is left for
Antonio's sojourn of fourteen years in the North,
his return to Venice, and death before 1406.

We will now pass on to another example of the
manner in which the truthfulness of Nicolò Zeno,
junior, is impugned by Admiral Zahrtmann. Most
geographers have heard of the famous collection of
Voyages and Travels made by the illustrious
Ramusio. Now because the Zeno narrative, which
was published in 1558, was not inserted in the first
edition of the second volume of Ramusio, published
in 1559, Admiral Zahrtmann would insinuate that
this showed a mistrust in Zeno's probity, but as
Ramusio died in 1557, it is difficult to see in what
earthly way this omission could imply any want of
confidence on his part.

" In the third edition of 1574, however," says Zahrtmann,
" the voyages are adopted to their full extent, together with
their splendid descriptions of the riches of Estotiland, which
last part of the story, however, it was thought fit to leave
out of the fourth edition, published in 1583, Frobisher having
in the meanwhile performed his voyages and, as we all know,
without finding any gold."

Now although Frobisher mistook Frisland for Greenland, and assumed the existence of a strait which his subsequent voyages showed to be a mistake, this was not Zeno's fault, and what Zahrtmann says of the consequent *alteration* in Ramusio is simply not the fact. Instead of the omission in the 1583 edition being an intentional one, as it would have been if it emanated from the editor, it is merely a case of a whole line, neither more nor less, having fallen out by the printer's carelessness, the full page in the 1574 and 1583 editions exactly tallying, with the exception that the former has 54 and the latter only 53 lines, in consequence of the accident in question. The absence of intention is shown by the utter nonsense, resulting from this omission, in the sequence of the language. The passage runs thus, the line in brackets being that which was printed in the previous edition of 1574 and in conformity with the Zeno text, but which has fallen out in the 1583 edition :—

"Hanno lingua e lettere separate, e cavano [metalli d'ogni sorte, é sopra tutto abondano d'oro, e le lor pratiche sono in Engroneland] di dove traggono pellerecie e zolfo e pegola." " They have a separate language and letters. They dig up [metals of every kind and abound in gold. Their commerce is with Greenland] whence they receive furs, brimstone, and pitch."

Let the reader join the two lines between which the omission occurs, and judge whether the editor of Ramusio adopted that mode of showing his mistrust of the Zeno narrative. It is true that Admiral Zahrtmann adopts this mare's nest from the words

of Mr. Biddle, the American author of the anonymous memoir of Sebastian Cabot, but it is difficult
to believe that one who was so anxious to show
that Ramusio mistrusted Zeno, and who was so intimately acquainted with the editions of Ramusio's
work, should not have had a copy of that work by
which he might verify the point for himself. One
thing is certain, that it was a bounden duty, both
in Biddle and Zahrtmann, before putting forth this
insinuation against the credit of Zeno, that each
should have made sure for himself that it was founded
on a right basis, whereas the reader has seen that
the proof of the exact contrary lay open to view on
the very surface.

Again : In 1533, when Nicolò was a young man
of eighteen, his grandfather Pietro was sent out to
Constantinople as ambassador from the Republic
to Sultan Soliman I, and Nicolò went with him.
Pietro's father, Caterino Zeno, had sixty years before
been sent out as ambassador to Persia, and on his
return his travels in Persia were printed, but in
his great-grandson's time this little pamphlet was
out of print. When Nicolò, therefore, was in Constantinople, he made a collection of rare books and
MSS., from which he was able to compile the
history of Caterino Zeno's embassy to Persia, which
was printed under the same cover with the narrative and map of the northern voyages now under
our notice. Admiral Zahrtmann considers it quite
incredible that Caterino Zeno's travels should have
been printed some sixty years before, and still not a

copy be procurable in Venice ; but as that fact had been stated in Ramusio as well as by Zeno, he lays before his readers a misinterpretation of the Italian words in one place, and suggests an alteration of the words in another, in order to fasten the assumed misstatement upon Zeno only. Fortunately, however, for the cause of accuracy, it will be recognized by any good Italian scholar, that the alteration which Admiral Zahrtmann proposes to make in the very simple sentence in Ramusio, is such as would certainly not be written by an Italian.

Admiral Zahrtmann's words are as follows :—

" Ramusio further mentions Catarino Zeno in terms of praise ; and, according to the statement of all authors who have treated of the subject, he regretted that he had not been able to procure a copy of his ' Travels in Persia', that work having become so rare, that in his time not a copy was to be found in Venice. This opinion is deduced from the following expressions of Ramusio :—' Così la fortuna ci fosse stata favorevole a farne venire nelle mani il viaggio del magnifico Mr Càtarino Zeno il Cavalier, che fù il primo ambasciatore ch' andava [andasse] in detta provinzia al Signore Ussumcassano ; ma la longhezza del tempo, auvegne che fossa [should be ' fosse'] stampato, ha fatto sì che l' habbiamo smarrito'—i.e., ' We were fortunate enough to get possessed of the Travels of the noble knight, Catarino Zeno, who was the first ambasador to Ussumcassan of Persia; but, although it was printed, the length of time has been the cause of our losing it.'

" In the above sentence there is, strictly speaking, no meaning ; for, the book being printed, could not surely make it more difficult to be lost by a collector like Ramusio, who in this case would naturally have taken notice of the remarkable circumstance that his missing copy was the last, and that not another was to be found—a thing that, with

lii   INTRODUCTION.

regard to time, place, and object, is quite incredible ; and
besides, if we were to suppose this to be the meaning of the
sentence, the construction would scarcely be correct, for
then the words 'auvegne che fossa stampata' [should be
'fosse stampato'] ought to have closed the period.

    "But if for 'auvegne' we substitute 'avanti', *i.e.*, 'before'
for 'although', the construction will be correct, and the
meaning of the sentence intelligible, though quite different
from that hitherto adopted.   The meaning will then be,
that the long time it took before Ramusio's own work got
printed caused him to lose the manuscript of Zeno's Voyage;
and this meaning is the more natural, as in reality the printing of his work encountered singular obstacles.   There
exist, for instance, editions of the first volume of the years
1550, 1554, 1563, 1588, and 1613 ; of the second, of 1559,
1564, 1574, and 1583 ; and of the third, of 1556, 1565, and
1606.   The reason of the third volume being published before the second is explained by Giunti, in his preface to the
second volume, by the death of Ramusio, and the burning
of his own printing office ; and it is precisely this volume
which contains the above-mentioned expressions of Ramusio.
If now it be permitted to suppose, in a posthumous work,
an error of the press so trifling, and, as it appears to me,
so likely to have occurred, the incredible assertion that the
account of Catarino Zeno's travels, performed in 1473,
should have been printed, and still not a copy to be procured in Venice, rests, in that case, solely on the testimony of Nicolò Zeno, his own great-grandson, who, as we
shall afterwards have occasion to see, was, as far back as
1533, employed under Catarino's son Pietro, and in that
situation occupied himself chiefly in collecting such accounts.
This appears to me not only incredible, but very suspicious."
—"Journal Roy. Geog. Soc.," vol. v, pp. 16, 17.

    The reader will have seen that Ramusio's language
instead of having "no meaning", was perfectly correct, and if any alteration from it, such as that sug-

gested by Admiral Zahrtmann, had been necessary,
it would, from the pen of an Italian, have taken the
shape not of " avanti che", but of " prima che". It
will be seen, however, that any such alteration would
be essentially wrong.

But having, by these means, invented a state of
things which never existed, Admiral Zahrtmann
comes to the following conclusion, which is here
given in his own words :—

" I am therefore led to the supposition that Ramusio did
not wish to admit this voyage into his collection, and that
he already mistrusted Nicolò Zeno's accounts of his ancestors."

Admiral Zahrtmann, however, was all this while
forgetting that Ramusio was dead a twelvemonth
before Zeno published anything at all, and could not
have exhibited any mistrust of a work that he never
saw; nor does it seem that his successors, whose words
Zahrtmann wrongly attributes to him and then mis-
translates, showed much mistrust in Zeno, when they
inserted in their work not only his own account of
Caterino's voyage to Persia, but his more remote ancestor's voyages to the North. These accounts of his
ancestors had gained for Nicolò Zeno the following
compliment from Francesco Patrizi :—" Sopra tutti
gli uomini maraviglioso Storico." " So extravagant
a praise," says Admiral Zahrtmann, " that it appears
to border on irony." Admiral Zahrtmann evidently
knew the peculiarities of the Italian people not more
intimately than he knew those of their language. In
commenting on Nicolò Zeno's account of Caterino's

travels, Zahrtmann says that it would be interesting to see it critically examined by an orientalist, in order to judge how far its details are to be relied upon. Surely the illustrious Giunti, the editors of Ramusio's work, might be relied on as a guarantee on this point, when after Nicolò Zeno's death they inserted in the same volume with Caterino's Embassy, four other contemporaneous voyages to Persia, viz.,— those of Angiolello, of Josafat Barbaro, of Ambrogio Contarini, and of an anonymous merchant, each one a check upon the historical credibility of the other. Lord Stanley of Alderley, no mean judge in such a case, has this year edited and annotated for our Society these very voyages, including that of Caterino Zeno, without taking any exception to its authenticity.

Again : Among the books which Nicolò Zeno bought when in Constantinople, was the biography of Carlo Zeno, the illustrious brother of our two northern travellers. This manuscript had been in the library of Matthias Corvinus, King of Hungary, and had been carried away by the Turks when they overran that country. Nicolò's purchase of this book leads Admiral Zahrtmann to say that

"It must naturally have appeared very surprising to Ramusio, that Nicolò Zeno should have had such uncommon good luck as to get possessed of all the most valuable documents concerning his own family."

This is as much as to say that the heir of a noble house is to be suspected of falsehood because he takes an interest in the history of his ancestors, and, when in the place most favourable for collecting such records, does not neglect the opportunity. "Though Ramusio," Zahrtmann says :—

"Perhaps did not think it prudent to express any surprise of this kind with reference to a person in Zeno's high station, I still think I trace in his above-mentioned expression a doubt in Zeno's veracity."

Admiral Zahrtmann then goes on to say that,—

" It may be inferred that similar doubts were entertained by others in Venice, from a book published there in 1576, by Tommaso Porcacchi da Castiglione, entitled 'L'isole piu famose del Mondo.' In this book the description of Iceland is taken from Olaus Magnus, and the map of it is copied from the chart of the Zeni. But as the Zeni themselves are not mentioned and no allusion is made to Frisland or their other discoveries, it is evident," says Zahrtmann, " that the author considered the voyages and discoveries of the Zeni as a fiction, and only with respect to Iceland preferred the Zeno chart to that of Olaus Magnus."

Now so far is this very unhandsome inference from being correct, that the facts adduced show that Porcacchi thereby gave the strongest proof in his power, consistently with the prudence and caution which an author owes to the integrity of his book, of the implicit reliance that he placed on the honour of the Zeno narrative, and the greater the prudence and caution on the one side, the greater the proof of confidence on the other. Porcacchi's book speaks exclusively of islands. Of the two most prominent in the Zeno map, viz.,—Frisland and Iceland, so little was known of the former, that it was not till two centuries afterwards that it was shown to mean the Færoe group. What wonder therefore that Porcacchi hesitated to deal with an island lying misty under

the veil of this mysterious name of Frisland, while
when treating of Iceland (of the existence of which
he had no doubt), he unhesitatingly adopts the
nomenclature supplied to him by the Zeno map? In
that nomenclature were included the names of the
Shetland Islands, which Nicolò Zeno by an unhappy
misreading had engrafted on the East Coast of Iceland; and when we find Porcacchi blindly accepting
these, and transferring them to his own book, can
we believe, what Zahrtmann says is *evident*, that he
considered the voyages and discoveries of the Zeni
were a fiction? Now Admiral Zahrtmann knew
very well, for he says so, that Frisland had not been
shown to represent the Færoe Islands till comparatively recent times, and he also knew, for he himself
says so, that the Færoe Islands themselves were so
little known in Nicolò Zeno's time, as not only not
to be recognizable in his Frisland, but not recognizable
from any previously published information: why
should he not, then, in all fairness, give Zeno
credit for having honourably produced his information, faulty as it may be, from the professed source,
to which only it can be traced; viz.,—the map laid
down by his ancestor from materials gathered in
his early visit to the locality itself? Instead of
this, Admiral Zahrtmann insinuates that Zeno had
in a great measure taken his materials from other
charts then in use. Here, again, Admiral Zahrtmann overreaches himself, for had this been the
case, Zeno would have become acquainted with the
group either under the correct name of Færoe Is-

lands, or that of Frislanda. If the former, he would have given it in the northern form in which he found it written down; if the latter, then it is clear that Frislanda was a recognizable name, and Zahrtmann's objection that it was not so falls to the ground.

Another of Admiral Zahrtmann's insinuations is that the exiled Archbishop of Upsala, Olaus Magnus Gothus, published at Venice, in 1539, a map of the three Scandinavian kingdoms, which Zahrtmann acknowledges that he had not seen,

"'As it appears doubtful whether any copy of it remains in existence."

Yet he says that :—

" It may very well have contained some information with respect to the general outline of Greenland, in which respect Zeno's chart is more correct than any known chart published before the sixteenth century."

That is to say that Zeno's excellent Greenlandic geography *may* have been derived from a map the contents of which nobody knows. But one thing Admiral Zahrtmann knew very well, for he says so, that the map which Olaus Magnus annexed to his brother Johannes Magnus' Gothic History, published in 1557 (which the editor has not seen), corresponds with that in Fickler's translation of Olaus Magnus' work, printed at Basle in 1567 (which the editor has seen), *yet neither one nor the other contains anything in common with the Zeno Map.* Did Olaus Magnus then repent himself of the excellencies of his map of 1539, and omit them in the later editions? Another of Admiral Zahrtmann's insinuations is,

that in the University Library of Copenhagen there
is a very old MS. map, in which the outline of
Greenland corresponds with that in Bordone's
"Isolario", published in Venice in 1526, 1534, and
1547, while the names agree almost uniformly with
those in Zeno's Greenland, and "the natural inference," he says, "is, that the original of this map has
served as a model to Bordone for his outline, and to
Zeno for his names." This suggestion of an original
to the Copenhagen MS. is very clever, as it draws off
attention from that MS. itself. But if said MS.
ever existed, why should it be supposed to have had
a predecessor in Italy unknown to northern geographers ? Being anxious to examine this point
thoroughly, the editor has endeavoured to procure a
photograph of this map from Copenhagen. At the
instance of a friend, the eminent poet Carl Andersen
(Inspector of the Royal Antiquarian Collection at
Rosenborg Palace) obligingly endeavoured for a whole
month to trace the fate of this map, but the following
is the reply : " The map is not to be found in the
Library, and must have been mislaid (or put away
and hidden) before the present head Librarian, Professor Thorsen, was appointed (I believe in 1833).[1] Two
years ago it was looked for, in consequence of a question propounded from America through the American
Minister, Dr. Cramer, but in vain, and this time
Professor Thorsen assures me they have made good
use of the time (a whole month), in which you have
been obliged to wait for an answer."

[1] The year in which Zahrtmann's Essay first appeared.

The non-appearance of this phantom of a map is unfortunate; but, as a matter of course, we take it for granted that Admiral Zahrtmann spoke of a veritable map, which from some cause is not recognized or is not forthcoming. That it bore no date is evident, but it is equally evident that a dateless map may have been made after, as well as before, 1558, and, *cæteris paribus*, there is quite as much reason to assume that its Greenland names were copied from Zeno's map, as the reverse. Now, let us see which is the more likely. Manuscripts do not, like printed books, visit us in our own homes, but, being preserved as treasures by their possessors, must be visited by those who wish to inspect them. No one yet ever heard of Nicolò Zeno, junior, having made a pilgrimage to Denmark for this or any other purpose, whereas his book and map, published in 1558, did travel north, as we know perfectly well, and produced a marked revolution in the notions of geographers in those countries. The editor claims, therefore, that Admiral Zahrtmann's argument falls utterly to the ground, while the evidence of probability lies entirely the other way.

Admiral Zahrtmann says that Zeno was so great a proficient in geography, that his own countrymen looked upon him as the greatest geographer of his time ; but here the writer in the North American Review, who was so impressed with Admiral Zahrtmann's " masterly production that he well nigh resolved to abandon the matter as beyond all hope of surgery", takes courage, and very justly says : " We shall not allow our nautical critic to blow hot and cold in the same breath; in one passage to give the noble Venetian the benefit of the respectability he enjoyed as a man of science, and in another, when it better suits the drift of his argument, to deny him the favourable estimation of learned men among his contemporaries." Of the estimation in which Nicolò Zeno was held for probity there can be no doubt. That his geographical knowledge may, for the period in which he lived, have been very respectable, is quite possible, and the really valuable map which came down to him from his ancestors may have enhanced his credit in that respect; but in very truth, he had no means from without, except the narrative, whereby to check the geography of the map, and none at all whereby to check his own misconceptions of the geography of the narrative.

After the affair in Shetland, Earl Sinclair left Nicolò Zeno in a fort which he had built at Bressay, with some small vessels, and men, and stores; and in the following summer, Zeno resolved to try his fortune in a voyage of discovery. He fitted out three small barks in the month of July, and sailing north, arrived in Engroneland or Greenland.

Here he found a monastery of Friars Preachers, and a church of St. Thomas, close by a volcanic hill. There was also a hot water spring, which the monks used for heating the church and the entire monastery, and by which they cooked their meat and baked their bread. By a judicious use of this hot water,

they raised in their small covered gardens the
flowers, fruits, and herbs of more temperate climates,
thereby gaining much respect from their neighbours,
who brought them presents of meat, chickens, etc.
They are indebted, the narrative says, to the volcano
for the very materials of their buildings, for by
throwing water on the burning stones while still hot,
they convert them into a tenacious and indestructible
substance, which they use as mortar. They have
not much rain, as there is a settled frost all through
their nine months' winter. They live on wild fowl
and fish, which are attracted by the warmth of that
part of the sea into which the hot water falls, and
which forms a commodious harbour. The houses are
built all round the hill, and are circular in form and
tapering to the top, where is a little hole for light
and air, the ground below supplying all necessary
heat. In summer time they are visited by ships from
the neighbouring islands and from Trondheim, which
bring them corn, cloths, and other necessaries in
exchange for fish and skins. Some of the monks are
from Norway, Sweden, and elsewhere, but most of
them from Shetland. The harbour is generally full
of vessels, detained by the freezing of the sea, and
waiting for the spring to melt the ice. The fishermen's
boats are like a weaver's shuttle; they are made of
the skins of fish, and sown together with fish bones
in such a manner, that, in bad weather, the fisherman can fasten himself up in his boat and expose
himself to the wind and sea without fear, for they
can stand a good many bumps without receiving any

injury. In the bottom of the boat is a kind of sleeve
tied fast in the middle, and when water gets into
the boat they put it into one half of the sleeve, close
it above with two pieces of wood and loose the band
beneath so that the water runs out. The friars are
liberal to workmen, and to those who bring them
fruit and seeds, so that many resort to them. Most
of the monks, especially the principals and superiors,
speak the Latin language. And this is all that is
known of Engroneland, as described by Messire
Nicolò Zeno.[1]

[1] This story of the monastery of St. Thomas, with its hot-water
conveniences, is assumed by a writer in the " Quarterly Review"
of October 1816, to be confirmed by the evidence of Dittmar Blefken, in his " Descriptio Islandiæ", published at Leyden in 1607.
12mo. Blefken has been supposed to be a German, but in the
absence of distinct authority for the supposition, I suspect, from
his name and the nature of his work, that he was a Dane. He
either visited, or pretended to have visited, Iceland in 1563. In
1565 he went to Lisbon and thence to Africa. Returning to Europe,
he sojourned some time at Venice with Count Otho. On the road
to Bonn he fell among robbers, who inflicted twenty-three wounds
on him, and plundered him of his MS. of the "Descriptio Islandiæ".
This MS. was re-discovered in Bonn in 1588, and published in
1607. Blefken states that he saw in the monastery of Helgafiel in
Iceland a blind monk, a Greenlander, who in his youth had been
placed by his parents in the monastery of St. Thomas in Greenland. He described the hot water as conducted by stone channels
from a boiling spring to the cells of the monks, and used both for
heating and cooking. The walls of the monastery were built of
pumice from a volcano hard by. The veracity of this work of Blefken's was indignantly attacked in 1612 by Arngrim Jonas, Pastor
of Mestland in Iceland and Provost of the neighbouring provinces,
a man of the highest repute among his countrymen, in a little
book, entitled " Anatome Blefkeniana, qua Ditmari Blefkenii vis-
cera, magis præcipua in Libello de Islandia, anno 1607 edito, con-

This interesting story brings us to the much vexed question of the site of the old Icelandic settlements in Greenland.

Until the first quarter of the present century the almost universal opinion was in favour of the east coast opposite Iceland. There was much to encourage this conclusion. The names of the two settlements, Ostrebygd and Westrebygd, easily led to the supposition that the former was seated on the east and the latter on the west coast of Greenland. The prevalent idea too, on the part of Icelanders in general, that this was the case, as well as certain expressions in

vulsa, per manifestam exenterationem retexuntur. Typis Holensibus in Islandia boreali." Anno 1612, 12mo. Inch by inch the asserted facts of Blefken's visit are disputed ; and, as regards his descriptive statements, Arngrim Jonas proves that he has stolen much without acknowledgment from Olaus Magnus and Sebastian Munster, and that what he has stated of his own, contains atrocious calumnies and astounding falsehoods. It might be objected that Arngrim Jonas being incensed against the author for aspersions on his country, may, in a spirit of contradiction, have made statements no more deserving of credit than Blefken's. His work is, however, preceded by a letter from the celebrated Gudbrand Thorláksson, Bishop of Hola, in Iceland, which confirms all Arngrim's points of evidence and condemns Blefken's work in the strongest terms of reprobation. Had I been able, by a critical observation of dates and facts, to have retained the testimony of Blefken as corroborative of Zeno, I should naturally have been but too glad to do so ; but the counter-evidence of these two worthy Icelanders, combined with the fact that the publication of the Zeno narrative in 1558 gave Blefken ample opportunity of seeing it, and availing himself of its contents, entirely deprives me of any inclination to trust to so frail a support. Moreover, I am satisfied that St. Olaus has been phonetically mistaken by Zeno for St. Tomaso.—R. H. M.

the ancient itineraries, when separately considered, seemed to lead very forcibly to the same conclusion. The story of the Icelandic colonisation of Greenland may be summarily stated as follows : In the beginning of the tenth century, Gunnbjorn, the son of Ulf Krake, a celebrated Norwegian rover, discovered at some distance due west from Iceland some large rocks, which he named after himself, Gunnbjornarsker ; and, in the same voyage, he also discovered still further to the west an extensive country, but on which he does not appear to have landed. No attempt to explore this region was made for a very long time, but the report of the discovery was preserved in Iceland, and at length Erick the Red, son of Thorward, a Norwegian Jarl, who, together with his father, had some years before been compelled to flee to Iceland, after his father's death was himself outlawed for murder, and resolved to seek the land which Gunnbjorn had seen, and promised to return with tidings if he discovered it. In 982 he sailed west from Sneefeldsnaes and found land, which from its height he called Midjokul, near the place afterwards known as Blaeserk or Blue Shirt. Thence he sailed along the shore in a southerly direction, seeking for the nearest habitable land. The first winter he passed in Erickseya, near the middle of what was afterwards called the Ostrebygd or eastern colony. The following year (A.D. 983) he came into Ericksfiord, where he fixed his abode. The same summer he explored the western desert and gave names to many places. In 985 he went to Iceland, and in the summer of 986 began to settle the land which he had discovered, which he called Greenland, because he said that the people would not like to move thither if the land did not have a good name. Colonists followed in considerable numbers, and the chiefs gave their own names to the bays and capes which they occupied, following the example of Erick, who dwelt at Brattahlid in Ericksfiord. In the year 999, Leif, Erick's son, sailed to Norway, and passed the winter at the court of king Olaus, who was zealous in propagating the Christian faith. Leif received baptism, and the next spring introduced Christianity into Greenland, taking with him a priest and several monks to Brattahlid. In course of time churches were built, and in the twelfth century the number of Christians had multiplied to such an extent, that they resolved to endeavour to obtain a bishop of their own, and in 1126 Bishop Arnold came to Greenland, and set up the episcopal seat at Gardar. From the Gripla we learn that Gardar was at the bottom of Ericksfiord, in the East Bygd, and there was a church there dedicated to St. Nicholas. There were twelve churches in the East Bygd and four in the West Bygd. The Episcopate continued till the beginning of the fifteenth century, Professor Finn Magnussen having shown that Andreas, the last Bishop, officiated in the Cathedral at Gardar in 1409 ; but after this period, communication with Norway and Iceland seems to have been almost entirely given up. An event, however, had occurred in 1349 of great interest to our subject, not only as regards the fate of the

*

colony, but the information with respect to its position, which we derive from a contemporary chronicler. In that year a descent was made by the Skrellings, or Esquimaux, upon the West Bygd, and it so happened that Ivar Bardsen, a Greenlander, who had been for many years steward or lay justiciary to the Bishop of Gardar, was sent to convey succour to the sister colony, and to drive away the Skrellings. He found, however, on arriving there, neither Christian nor heathen, but only some cattle running wild, which his people took on board their vessels and returned home. Of this occurrence, Ivar Bardsen has himself left a record in a document of very great importance, of which more will have to be said presently.

There is yet another document extant, which throws light upon the subsequent fate of the abandoned colonists. A letter of Pope Nicholas V to the Bishops of Skalholt and Holar in Iceland, dated 1448, discovered by Professor Mallet early in this century in the Papal Archives, tells us that the Christians had maintained for many centuries the Christian faith, established by King Olaf in Greenland, and had erected many churches and a cathedral, until, about thirty years ago (*i.e.*, about 1418), some heathens from the neighbouring coasts came upon them with a fleet, and laid waste the country and its holy buildings with fire and sword, sparing nothing but the small distant parishes, which they were prevented from reaching by the intervening mountains and precipices. The inhabitants of both sexes they carried away into slavery. What became of the remnant of the colony of the East Bygd is a mystery. Either like their brethren of the West Bygd, they may have been exterminated by the Skrellings, or may have mingled with the Esquimaux, and adopted their manners and customs. At any rate, the consequence was that Greenland was for a long time forgotten, until at the beginning of the sixteenth century, Erick Walckendorf, Archbishop of Trondheim, took pains to collect together all the ancient accounts concerning it that he could, and submitted to the government a proposition for the re-discovery of the lost colony. Unfortunately, however, before his plan was developed, he fell into disgrace with the King, and was banished to Rome, but subsequently died at Amsterdam, in 1523. Since his time a great many expeditions have been sent out by the Kings of Denmark in search of the colony. In the reign of Frederick II, Magnus Heinesen went out in 1578. In the long reign of Christian IV, from 1588 to 1648, were sent out the expeditions of Godske Lindenow, and Carsten Rickardsen, and Jens Munk; but all these attempts were fruitless, as far as concerned the discovery of Greenland to the East of Cape Farewell. The voyages of David Danell, in the reign of Frederick III, however, furnish some useful data about the East Coast. At length, in the beginning of the eighteenth century, Hans Egede, a Norwegian clergyman, regardless of ridicule or hardship, persuaded Frederick IV to send him out as the missionary priest of a new colony to be established in Greenland. His judicious conduct secured him the confidence of the natives of the West Coast; but being convinced that they could not be descendants of Europeans, he determined on visiting the East Coast, and set out for that purpose with two barges on the 9th August, 1723, but for want of sufficient necessaries was obliged to put back on reaching lat. 60° 20′. Between the 60th and 61st degrees of latitude he discovered at Kakortok, in what is now called Julianashaab, a remarkable ruin which proved that the Icelanders had formerly been there. (See View, p. 49.) In 1728 Major Paars and Captain Landorf were ordered to ride on horseback from the West Coast to the East, but, as may be supposed, with little success. In 1752 Peter Olsen Valloe with four other Europeans in a Greenland skin-boat explored several of the fjords in the district of Julianashaab, and gave a description of some of the many ruins to be found there. He succeeded in reaching the southern shores of the East Coast in Lat 60° 28′. The expeditions of Lôvenörn in 1786 and of Paul Egede and Rothe in 1787 were equally unsuccessful in attaining the desired object. Not more successful than the Danish voyagers were our own great navigators, Davis, Hudson, and others, who aimed at the solution of this problem. The attempt to approach the land on the East appears to have been abandoned as hopeless, until Captain Scoresby showed that even in such high latitudes as between 70° and 75° N., the coast was not altogether unapproachable. Indeed, Scoresby effected more for geographical science in a few days than had been done in that direction for centuries. His voyage

appears to have been the stimulus which roused the
Danish Government to the exertion of sending out a
very able naval officer, of perseverance, intelligence
and courage, not exceeded by the most enterprising
officers of any country. Captain Graah sailed from
Copenhagen the 31st March, 1828, and returned in
September, 1831, but it was not till 1837 that
we were able to read in English that excellent
narrative with which most of us are so well acquainted.

The now well known fact that the ruins of churches
and other buildings have been found in the district
of Julianashaab, on the south-west coast of Greenland,
may lead some to suppose that the question is thereby
settled; but it should be remembered that there is
nothing in the ruins themselves, apart from the testimony of ancient documents, to show that they may
not have been those of the West Bygd, whereas the
point at issue is the site of the East Bygd, far
and away the more important of the two, and the
seat of the bishoprick. It is true that Captain Graah
believed the East Bygd to have been situated in
Julianashaab, and laboured to prove it, but the
editor can conscientiously assert that, after a careful
study of his book, he was still of opinion that the
East Bygd was on the East Coast; and that he was
not the only one unconvinced by Captain Graah's
arguments, will be seen by the following quotation
from a valuable work, entitled " Iceland, Greenland,
and the Faroe Islands", published in 1844, by Harper,
of New York :—

"The voyage of Graah, which has been regarded as settling the dispute, is by no means decisive. The difficulties he had to encounter prevented him from surveying the shores with the requisite accuracy, and the interior of the fiords where the ruins of the colony might be expected to occur, were almost unvisited. Moreover, he himself acknowledges that before going out he was 'thoroughly convinced that the Eastbygd would not be found on the east coast', a state of mind not the best fitted to ensure success, or encourage exertion. While these things lessen the value of his evidence against its existence on the eastern coast, some facts stated by him tend rather to favour the opposite conclusion."

And, after having well weighed Captain Graah's arguments, he says :—

"For these reasons we are disposed to regard this point not only as still undecided, but one on which, without more evidence, it would be premature to come to any conclusion."

It will have been observed that the editor has not allowed himself to pause upon the details of any of those explorations, which occupied some three centuries, and with good reason. The point in dispute has not been an object of inquiry for the keel and the compass only, but also for the pen, and Danes and Icelanders have for centuries studied old Sagas and chorographies, in the hope of arriving by dint of comparison, analysis, and digestion at the solution of a mystery which seemed always to slip away from the grasp of certainty ; and yet the whole of that time they had the best possible means of settling the question within their possession.

That same Ivar Bardsen, so many years steward or justiciary to the bishopric of Gardar in the East

Bygd, was sent out by the bishop with succours to the West Bygd when the latter was attacked by the Skrellings. Now this man has left us sailing directions for reaching the East Bygd, both from Bergen in Norway, and from Iceland, and he has also left us a chorography of Greenland itself; and as he was himself a Greenlander, and long a resident in the East Bygd, knowing perfectly all the places of which he speaks, the editor holds his testimony to be of the highest value and not to be lightly disputed.

There is in Purchas a copy of this document in English, the result of many translations, which belonged to Henry Hudson. It was translated from a German translation into Dutch by William Barentz. The Dutch belonged to Peter Plancius, who lent it to Hudson, and he had a fresh translation made into English expressly for himself. A more interesting group of names in connection with one document could scarcely be produced. Fortunately, the learned Danish Professor C. C. Rafn has given us in his extremely valuable "Antiquitates Americanæ", published in Copenhagen (1837, 4to), the text of an early copy of the document found in the Færoe Islands, with a Latin translation, by which the editor has been able to correct the defects of Hudson's mongrel copy.

Captain Graah, of whose gallantry as an explorer and ability as a writer the editor would never willingly speak without the deepest respect, is scarcely consistent when he speaks of this valuable document. He at one time says that " the Chorography of Ivar

*

Bardsen is the only one we can at all depend on in deciding the position of the Ostrebygd" (see p. 155); and when he mistakenly supposes that it does not sufficiently answer his purpose, he says (p. 175), that

" His sailing directions are at best apocryphal; that they have been written down from oral tradition, and collected and put together by Archbishop Walkendorf a century after all intercourse with Greenland had ceased."

The editor is reluctantly obliged to say that this assertion is not compatible with common sense. How could oral traditions, collected by Archbishop Walkendorf in 1516, be made to be one and the same thing with a consecutive description of the topography of the country more ample in detail than any other that exists, derived from Ivar Bardsen, who flourished in the fourteenth century, and which, as will be presently shown, proves the East Bygd to be on the south-west coast, while Walkendorf and all those whom he consulted were convinced it was on the east coast?

It is, moreover, stated in Purchas (ff. 520, 521), that his text was taken in 1596 from an old book of accounts in the Færoe Islands written above a hundred years before, which was earlier by twenty years than the period of Walkendorf's collection, and Rafn tells us (*Antiq. Am.*, p. 301), that the Purchas version was based upon a very ancient copy of the original which had contained some correct readings. That Archbishop Walkendorf would get the best copy he could we cannot doubt, and that copy Rafn has adopted and printed with a Latin translation from the Danish, and from his Latin the editor has made his translation, but has given in an appendix both the Danish and the Latin texts.

Captain Graah has given us another very remarkable proof that his critical treatment of Ivar Bardsen cannot be blindly accepted. In his sailing directions Ivar Bardsen tells us that,

"In sailing from Iceland to Greenland, you first shape your course due west till you come to Gunnbiorn's Skerries, which lie midway between Iceland and Greenland, and in the ancient times this westerly course was followed to Greenland, but now the ice has drifted down from the north, and set itself fast so near to Gunnbiorn's Skerries, that none without peril of life can follow it. You then sail to the south-west until you have got past all the ice lying at and about Gunnbiorn's Skerries, and must then steer to the north-west for a day and a night, which will bring you to Hvarf."

On this downward drifting of the ice Captain Graah remarks (p. 158),

"This can scarcely have been the real cause, for the ice along the east coast of Greenland was in all likelihood much the same in the tenth century as it was in the fourteenth and is now."

This, to the editor, unintelligible remark, reads oddly by the side of the following expression of the Danish hydrographer, Admiral Zahrtmann.

"We learn," he says, "from Captain Graah,[1] that the ice is continually on the increase along this coast, thereby necessitating its thin population to emigrate to the west side, where this increase of ice and decay of the monuments of antiquity are also keeping pace together."

[1] "Royal Geographical Society's Journal," vol. v, p. 102.

Having thus disposed of the ice round Gunnbiorn's Skerries, Captain Graah dealt with the Skerries themselves in the following manner. Not finding them where Ivar Bardsen places them, midway between Iceland and Greenland, he says that

"The fact is disproved not only by the experience of the Icelandic traders and fishermen, but by that also of the English and Dutch whalers,"

and, *proprio motu*, he applied the name of Gunnbiorn's Skerries to some small rocks close off the coast of Greenland, in lat. 65° 30', an artificial mode of making Ivar Bardsen's sailing directions lead to the site where Captain Graah assumed the East Bygd to lie. By such a route to Julianashaab, it is clear that Captain Graah cannot claim to be following the guidance and authority of Ivar Bardsen, but simply his own conclusions. These conclusions, though very natural, threw discredit on the value of Ivar Bardsen's guidance, and yet, as we shall see, Ivar Bardsen was a faithful guide who would have led him unerringly to the desired spot.

Gunnbiorn's rocks, to have answered Ivar Bardsen's description, could have been of no insignificant size, and yet it is quite true that they were not to be seen where Ivar Bardsen places them. Captain Graah, therefore, was in no sense to blame for the conclusion that he came to, but at the same time Ivar Bardsen was not at fault either. It has been the editor's good fortune to make the discovery of a fact with which neither Captain Graah nor any of the disputants in this case have been in the slightest

degree acquainted, but which entirely vindicates the
integrity of Ivar Bardsen's directions, and will, it is
hoped, help to remove from the long vexed question
of the site of the East Bygd, those remains of doubt
which Captain Graah, with all his great merits, has
still allowed to rest on the minds of many on this
subject.

In the 1507 edition of Ptolemy is a most valuable
map of the world, made by a German named Johann
Ruysch, a map which would be eminently remarkable as an engraved map if only for its very early
date, but it is pre-eminently so from the fact that it
is the first engraved map on which America is laid
down. Now, for more than a quarter of a century
the editor has been aware of the fact that on this
map was a legend recording the destruction by a
volcanic eruption, at an early date, of an island
somewhere up in the north, and he recollects
many years ago pointing out the fact to Sir John
Richardson ; but no special line of study had at
that time led him to the recognition of what
this island might be. When, however, the subject
of which he is now treating began seriously to
occupy his attention, the existence of this legend
came back to his memory, and, on recurring to the
old map, he found midway between Iceland and
Greenland, as Ivar Bardsen had described the position of Gunnbiorn's Skerries, though rather nearer
to Iceland than to Greenland, a large island, against
which stood this inscription—"Insula hæc anno
Domini 1456 fuit totaliter combusta." " This island

in the year of our Lord 1456 was entirely blown up"; and, in confirmation of the fact, the editor found on later maps the shoal formed by the remains of the explosion laid down in precisely the same locality with the name of "Gombar Scheer", a name which it is impossible not to recognise as a sailor's version of Gunnbiorn's Skerries.

On one of these maps, entitled "Pascaert van Groenlandt", by Jan van Keulen, without a date, but about 1700, the editor had the pleasure to find soundings on the reef. The shoal was represented as *full sixty miles* long from north to south, and about twenty-five miles broad from east to west. The soundings at the north and south ends were both twenty-five fathoms, while the nearest soundings northwards were seventy, eighty, and one hundred fathoms. It has been stated, that while this shoal lies essentially in the position described by Ivar Bardsen, midway between Iceland and Greenland, it is, if anything, somewhat nearer to Iceland, a fact which will, the editor conceives, from a nautical point of view, give additional weight to the correctness of Ivar Bardsen's directions ; for the more easterly the point at which the sailor began to set his south-west course, the more likely would he be, under the influence of the strong south-west current, to make sufficient southing to bring his vessel into a position to make Cape Farewell by a subsequent tack to the north-west.

But now that Ivar Bardsen's sailing directions are restored to their integrity, let us see what his chorography says. Of course only such extracts are given as are necessary. He brings us by sea to a Highland named Hvarf, a word which means a turning point, and is the same word which, in the north of Scotland, has taken the shape of Cape Wrath. From this point Ivar Bardsen takes us first eastwards, and by long leaps brings us to two fiords, quite uninhabited, named respectively Berefiord and Oellum-lengri, which means "the longest of all." It is so long that he says, "no one ever saw the end of it." It may very easily be Franz Joseph Fiord, which Lieut. Payer, in Captain Koldewey's expedition in the *Germania* in 1870, ascended for seventy miles, and then from the top of a peak 7,000 feet high, saw it still stretching indefinitely westward. "Further to the East", Ivar Bardsen says,

"Is a great mountain of ice named Finnsbuda, and further still an island named Kaarsoe, beyond which nothing can be seen on sea or land but ice and snow."

He then brings us back to his starting point Hvarf, and thence leads us westwards, describing *seriatim* the different fiords and localities in the East Bygd, about whose names there is no manner of doubt, as several of them are mentioned in the Sagas and the other chorographies. And now what follows is deserving of special notice. After leading us from place to place gradually westwards to a fiord called Ericksfiord, he says

"*Northwards* from Ericksfiord are two arms of the sea named Ydrevig and Indrevig. Next, *northwards*, lies Brede-

⁂

fiord ; thence, *further to the north*, is Eyrarfiord ; and so on
to Isefiord, which is the most westerly fiord in the East
Bygd."

He then says that, between the East and the
West Bygds, was a space of twelve nautical miles of
entirely uninhabited country, and finishes his chorography by saying, that the West Bygd had been
utterly depopulated by the Skrellings.

Now it does not need much reflection to see that
this series of places running westwards from Hvarf
cannot possibly be on the east coast, for let us place
Hvarf on that coast wherever we may,—say, for
argument's sake, where the old Icelanders conjectured
that it lay, in about lat. 63 deg.,—every step we then
take to the west, *i.e.*, to our left hand, leads us more
and more to the south, while Ivar Bardsen makes
the last-named places in the series go more and more
to the north. It is needless to say that on the west
coast the case is exactly reversed. If, therefore, we
take Hvarf to be, as its name would suggest, the
" turning point" of the east and west coasts, the
description is in harmony not only with common
sense, but with the real trending of the land first
west, then north, as later geographical research has
shown it to be, and thus, beyond all question, we
have the East Bygd in the district of Julianashaab,
where Captain Graah, by more circuitous but less
conclusive processes, strove to prove it to be.

This simple exposition is the editor's strong point
for the final settlement of the site of the East Bygd,
and he believes it to be unanswerable. It may not

unreasonably be regarded as a matter of surprise that an argument so conclusive as this should have escaped the attention of all the distinguished commentators who have sought the solution of this question, from Archbishop Walkendorf in 1516, and the learned Torfæus, downwards to the present day. A higher authority than Ivar Bardsen could not possibly be desired; a more explicit and lucid description could not be wished ; the conclusion from it is utterly inevitable ; and yet Captain Graah himself, whose whole heart and soul were in the subject, and whose very words are " that the chorography of Ivar Bardsen is the only one we can at all depend on in this matter", wrote a most able and learned appendix of twenty-one octavo pages in small type to prove his point by ingenious and very reasonable arguments on the application of almost every other ancient passage but the one which would have placed unanswerable demonstration between his fingers.

It may be suggested that in the sixteenth and seventeenth centuries, they had no maps sufficiently trustworthy to help them to such a conclusion. There remains, however, another process of reasoning, equally simple, which leads to the same result without the need of a map. If the series of places *eastwards* from Hvarf brings us to where " one can go no further for the ice and snow", which are characteristics of the north, and if the series of names *westwards* terminates also with places more and yet more to the north, it stands to reason that Hvarf itself must be a point at the south between the two,

*

and, consequently, the East Bygd, by Ivar Bardsen's showing, must of necessity have lain immediately to the west of the southern point of Greenland. Although neither of these lines of thought seems ever to have occurred to any commentator for the last 360 years, they are not the less conclusive for all that.

And now let us see how far Ivar Bardsen's and Zeno's descriptions are confirmative of each other.

After enumerating a few places west of Hvarf, Ivar Bardsen brings us to a place called Petersvig, near which is a great monastery dedicated to St. Olaus and St. Augustine. He also says that

"In the inner recess of a neighbouring fiord called Rafnsfiord is a cloister of Sisters of the order of St. Benedict. Within the bay are some small islands half belonging to the cloister and half to the cathedral. These islands abound in water, so hot in winter as to be unapproachable, but in summer temperate enough to be used for washing and for the healing of the sick."

We have a corroboration of this fact in the hot springs of Ounartok, near which some remains of the buildings of the old colonists have been found. Captain Graah, who visited these, tells us that there are three springs close by one another at the north-east corner of the island of Ounartok. The one nearest the sea is insignificant, its temperature being only 26 deg. of Reaumur (91 deg. Fahrenheit). The second, a few paces from it, forms a lake of about 48 feet in circuit ; its temperature was 27 deg. (93 deg. Fahrenheit). The third is still larger, being about 70 feet in cir-

cuit, and its temperature from 32 to 33½ Reaumur
(104 to 108 Fahrenheit). The Greenlanders state
that the water is much hotter in winter than in summer: an effect which probably arises from the air being
much colder in winter, and the contrast accordingly
more perceptible. This must be acknowledged to be,
incidentally at least, a very remarkable confirmation
by the old Greenlander, of Zeno's interesting story of
the monastery. That he makes no reference to the
ingenious applications of the hot water need occasion
no surprise, for they may not have existed at the
time when he wrote, which was considerably before
Zeno's period; and even if they did, they were items
of detail which would not necessarily be inserted in a
mere chorography. The difference between the
names of St. Olaus and St. Tomaso, given by the
two to the same monastery, is easily explainable.
The northern name of St. Olaf would be as strange
as Sanscrit to the mind of the Venetian, and its
Latinised form of St. Olaus would sound to his ear
like nothing so much as San Tomaso. As regards
his describing the monks as Dominicans instead of
Augustinians, we have no alternative but to accept
it as a misapprehension on his part, bearing no influence upon the question either one way or the
other.

Professor Rafn, to whose learning and untiring
industry we are so deeply indebted for the great
amount of enlightenment that we now possess on
the movements of the old Scandinavians in Greenland,
has endeavoured to fix the localities of the ancient

settlements on the face of a modern map, and, as far as may be judged from Ivar Bardsen's chorography taken by itself, the Professor's map appears most admirably and judiciously drawn up. A sketch map of the district from a Danish Admiralty Chart corrected to 1871, with Rafn's adaptation of the ancient names, is here given. When, some months since, the editor read before the Royal Geographical Society the more purely geographical portions of this investigation, he was easily tempted to conclude that the hot springs referred to by Ivar Bardsen, which seemed to tally with those of Ounartok, visited and described by Captain Graah, were also identical with the sources of the hot water used in the monastery described by Zeno. Subsequent reflection has caused him to alter this opinion. The only monastery mentioned by Ivar Bardsen is the Augustinian one dedicated to St. Olaus, and as far as the editor is able to form an opinion from Ivar Bardsen's chorography alone, he sees no reason to differ from the conclusion of Professor Rafn, who places its site near the lake which lies on the right hand side of the inner recess of the Fjord of Tessermuit, in lat. 60 deg. 26 min., in almost the same latitude, it is true, as Ounartok, but separated therefrom by two fjords, at the mouth of the second of which Ounartok lies. Moreover, the description of the islands of Ounartok does not tally with that of the site of the monastery, which, according to Ivar Bardsen, was near a lake, a condition realised in the position adopted by Rafn.

It is true that Dr. Rink, the late Inspector of

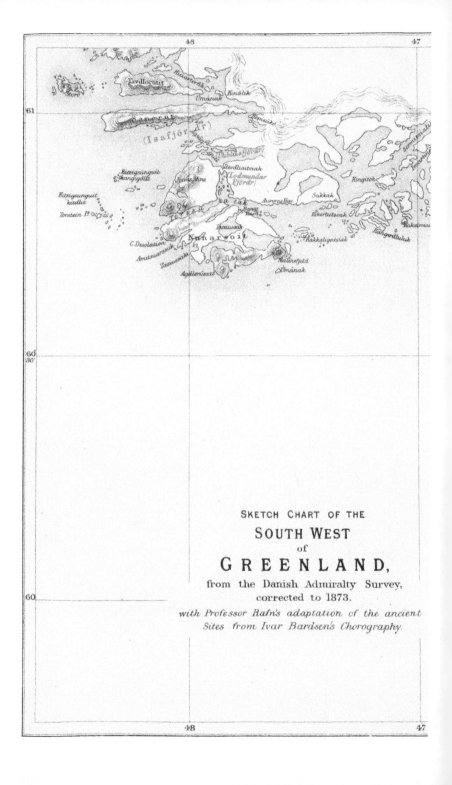

SKETCH CHART OF THE

SOUTH WEST

of

GREENLAND,

from the Danish Admiralty Survey,
corrected to 1873.

with Professor Rafn's adaptation of the ancient
Sites from Ivar Bardsen's Chorography.

Igdlo

Sermilik

Kangeitsiak

Ukivisokak

(Breidifiord)

Narsak

(Tunnudliorbik)

(Brattahl

(Burfjeld)

Nook

Eriksoe

Iglupalik

(Isaldar)

(Dalr)

Akugnek

Tuktotok

Igdlokasik

Kakortok

(Finarsfjord)

Kangerdluarsok

Alge Umik

Karmânguak

Kingaitsok

Ringiglok

Simiatot

Skovfjord

Nakarnak

Julianeshaab

Hvidenæs

Irsarut

Kilangak

Akia

Omenalik

Kudlyk

Hollander Hav

Paradiis

Igdlosualsiak

Omanak

Ûmanak

Upernavik

Iulissatsiak

Sardlok

Kuersok

Lichtenau

Kingigtok

Ûmânârssuk

Kekertarssuak

Ujaragtarfit

S. Proven

Takat

Omenartot

Arnat

(Kaf

Imarudligak

Kikertarsoitsiak

Nev

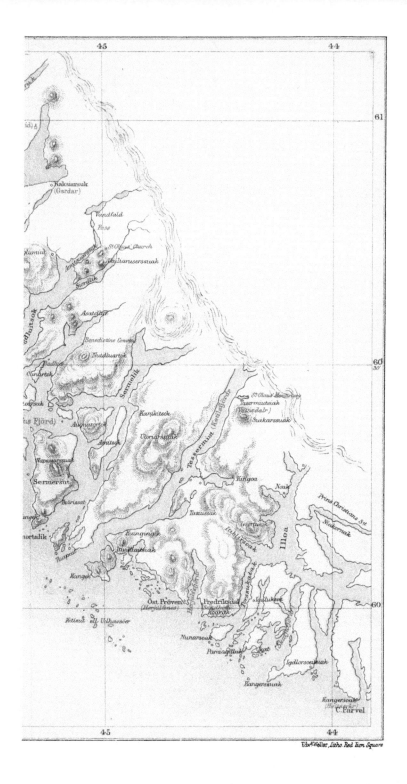

South Greenland, has obligingly written to inform the
editor that he knows of no hot springs in the district
of Julianashaab, besides those of Ounartok; but there
is enough capriciousness in volcanic action to make
that fact far from conclusive as to the non-existence
of hot springs in another proximate locality five
centuries ago. Moreover, there is a remarkable ex-
plicitness in the description of a phenomenon which
our knowledge in the present day shows to be perfectly accurate. The text says that

" Where the warm water falls into the sea there is a large
and wide harbour, which, from the heat of the boiling water,
never freezes all the winter, and the consequence is that
there is such an attraction for sea-fowl and fish, that they
are caught in unlimited quantity."

In this description we have a picture of far greater
volume and activity in the hot spring than is conveyed by Captain Graah's description of the shallow
pools, nowhere deeper than a foot, at Ounartok.
Yet this volume and this activity of the thermal
spring are requisite for the effect described, viz., the
attraction of the fish, so that we are compelled to
assume the former existence of a spring near the
monastery, now no longer known.

The mention of the employment of the pumice and
calcareous tufa in constructing buildings, and making
the mortar which bound them together, would also
seem to imply greater abundance of material than
could be looked for in the pools at Ounartok. In any
case we cannot but regard the account of the monastery as one of those " descriptions détaillées d'objets

dont rien en l'Europe ne pouvoit leur avoir donné
l'idée", for which Humboldt commends the Zeno
narrative : while the existence of the Ounartok hot
springs in the neighbourhood at the present day,
and the mention of such hot springs by Ivar Bardsen
about the same locality, are evidences quite sufficient
to warrant our acceptance of the credibility of the
Zeno account. But the monastery was not only
near a lake according to Ivar Bardsen, but according
to Zeno it was near a hill which vomited fire like
Vesuvius and Etna, and whether it be an extinct volcano or not, there is on the Danish map, in a position
corresponding with that fixed by Rafn, a hill named
Suikärssuak. Closely connected with this subject is
one to which the editor, at page xxvi of this introduction, promised to recur. It is to be noticed that both
in the map and in the narrative there are two names,
" Grolanda", or " Grolandia", and " Engronelanda",
which the text shows to mean only one country. On
page 34, the word Grolanda is applied by Antonio
Zeno to the country discovered by his brother
Nicolò, and on page 12 that same country is called
Engronelanda, and we have the clearest possible proof
in the Zeno map, that that country is Greenland.
From the extract from Antonio Zeno's letter, page
34, we gather that the remarkable delineation of
Greenland on the map is derived from Sinclair, since
the language takes the following shape :

" I have written the life of my brother, the Chevalier,
Messire Nicolò, with the discovery which he made, and all
about Grolanda. I have also written the life and exploits

of Zichmni, a prince as worthy of immortal memory as any that ever lived for his great bravery and remarkable goodness. In it I have described the *discovery of Engroniland on both sides and the city that he founded.*"

The combination of these two expressions in one sentence leads to the inference that the discovery of Greenland on both sides was due to Sinclair. On page xxvi of this introduction, the editor wrote as follows :

"Those portions of the ancient story which have not been marred by misreading, exaggeration, or unintelligent interference, are, *with one exception*, which will be spoken of hereafter, in harmony with the knowledge which we possess in the present day."

We now come to speak of that exception. As has been just said, in the description of Nicolò Zeno's visit to Greenland it is stated (p. 12), that "he found a monastery *hard by a hill, which vomited fire like Vesuvius and Etna*", and then the account goes on to speak of the spring of hot water, with which the church of the monastery and the chambers of the friars were heated. Now although we know of thermal springs in Greenland, and in the very district which has been demonstrated to be the site of the ancient colony, we have never heard of any active volcano there. Nevertheless, we have at the close of this very narrative a corroboration from an independent source of this statement respecting a volcano. When Sinclair reached Greenland, after his adventure off Ireland (see text, pp. 26-31), he entered a harbour, from which, Antonio says, " we saw in the distance a great mountain that

*

poured forth smoke." The harbour they called Trin, and whether rightly or wrongly, that is to say, whether so standing on the old map or inserted haphazard by Nicolò Zeno, junior, the promontory of Trin is placed at the extreme south point of Greenland. A hundred soldiers sent out from the harbour of Trin to explore the country, returned after eight days, and brought word that

"They had been up to the mountain, and that the smoke was a natural thing proceeding from a great fire in the bottom of the hill, and that there was a spring from which issued a certain matter like pitch, which ran into the sea."

This two-fold testimony to the existence at that time of a volcano in the south of Greenland, of which we know nothing at the present day, seems to place the subject out of the range of those puzzles which have originated from Nicolò Zeno, junior's, misreading or misapprehension. Although no one yet, as far as the editor is aware, has detected the existence in this locality of either an active or an extinct volcano, it must be conceded that in a country like Greenland the existence of an extinct volcano may very easily elude observation, both from the denudation of its peak by glacial action, and from the snow and ice concealing what lies below them. Meanwhile, the known existence of thermal springs in the neighbourhood favours the reasonableness of our accepting as accurate the two statements of the text.

So much for the confirmation of Zeno by Ivar Bardsen ; we now come to the confirmation of Ivar Bardsen by Zeno. In spite of all the ridiculous blunders implanted on it by Nicolò Zeno, junior, from misreadings of the narrative, the Zeno map was based on a genuine old map made by his ancestor. As such it is a most remarkable phenomenon in geographical history, for it contains geography, far in advance not only of what was generally known at the time when it was first laid down in the fourteenth century, but in advance even by generations of what was known at the time of its publication in the sixteenth century. The approximate accuracy in the delineation of Greenland under the name of Engroneland has been the subject of repeated notice. The reader's attention is invited to the word " Avorf" on that map near its south point. It is a valuable word, for it proves a very great deal. There can be no doubt that it is the " Hvarf" of Ivar Bardsen and all the chorographies. In fact, in Bjorn Jonsen's chorography, where it is spelt " Hafhvarf", the identity is still more apparent. Near it also is the name of "Af Prom", which is doubtless a second mode of writing the same thing, viz., the promontory of Hvarf, by the maker of the old map. The position of this name on this map is a most remarkable evidence from a quarter where one would least expect it; viz., from the chance visit of a Venetian to the spot at the close of the fourteenth century, of the true site of the lost East Bygd. Its spelling is another example of the mode in which a northern word can be represented by a southerner, and its accordance with the native description of Ivar Bardsen is another proof of Nicolò Zeno, junior's, ignorant reading of the text when he places the convent of St. Thomas in the preposterous position in which we see it, on the remotest shores of the Frozen Ocean. Having first mistaken Bres, or rather Bressay, where his ancestor's brother wintered in the Shetland Islands, for a place in Iceland, and finding that in the spring he goes north to Engroneland, he places him up there.[1]

Another notable fact is that, in the Zeno map, all the settlements lie on the west and not on the east coast. While, therefore, these facts corroborate Ivar Bardsen's chorography and the site of the East Bygd derived therefrom, they also, in the most conclusive manner, prove the genuineness of the original narrative and map of the Zeno, and that the chief cause of the doubt of their authenticity has been Nicolò Zeno, junior's, blundering readings of the narrative represented upon the face of the map. This being so, we find ourselves in possession of an interesting description of the prosperous condition of the East Bygd, between the period of the destruction of the West Bygd and its own disappearance from man's knowledge, which we possess in no other document what-

---

[1] One of Admiral Zahrtmann's insinuations, entirely unsupported by evidence, is that Nicolò Zeno may have derived from priests in Rome information about Greenland which they had received from Archbishop Walkendorf during his exile. It is not likely, for Walkendorf died in Amsterdam when Zeno was eight years old. His main object was to learn the way to the East Bygd, and Ivar Bardsen's directions and chorography stood first and most important among the documents that he secured. If, then, Nicolò Zeno by any process gained possession of Walkendorf's information, it was quite impossible that he should place the monastery of St. Thomas where he has done on the map.

ever. The description of the fishermen's boats and
their contrivances for safety in those dangerous seas,
is truly admirable. The mode of constructing their
houses in this strange country, related to us by an
eye-witness, five hundred years ago, and the use of
potstone, a true Greenlandic product, in their domestic utensils, have about them an interest of a very
rare character ; and the plan of heating their dwell-
ings and cooking their victuals with the water of
the natural hot springs, is but a curious early example of what has been done in later times at Chaudes
Aigues, in the department of Cantal, where the water
from the Par fountain conveys heat to some hun-
dreds of houses, and is made otherwise serviceable
for domestic purposes.

After the death of Nicolò, Sinclair would not
allow Antonio to return to Venice, but being determined to make himself lord of the sea, wished to
send him out to the westwards to verify the report
of some fishermen who had discovered some rich and
populous countries in that direction, which we shall
presently see to be America. The narrative, which
was embodied in a letter from Antonio to his brother
Carlo, is in brief as follows.

Six and twenty years ago four fishing boats put
out to sea, and encountering a heavy storm were
driven over the sea in utter helplessness for many
days, and at length came to an island called Estotilanda, lying one thousand miles west of Frislanda.
One of the boats was wrecked, and its crew of six
men were brought by the natives into a large and

populous city and taken before the chief, who sent
for many interpreters to speak with them. Only one
of these, who spoke Latin and had also been cast by
chance upon the island, could understand them. On
learning who they were and where they came from,
the chief desired that they should stay in the country, which they did perforce for five years, and learned
the language. One of them in particular having
seen much of the island, reported that it was rather
smaller than Iceland, but much more fertile, having
in the middle a high mountain, whence flow four
rivers which water the whole country. The inhabitants are very intelligent, and possess many arts.
In the king's library were found several Latin books
which were not at that time understood. The people
had their own language and letters, and in the
south there was a great and populous country very
rich in gold. Their foreign intercourse was with Engroneland, whence they imported furs, brimstone, and
pitch. They sowed corn and made beer, which is "a
kind of drink that north people take as we do wine".
They had woods of immense extent and many towns
and villages. They built small boats and sailed them,
but knew nothing of the compass. Hence these
fishermen were held in high estimation, and were
sent southwards with twelve boats to a country
called Drogio. They arrived there after a perilous
voyage, but, the inhabitants being cannibals, most of
the crews were eaten. The fisherman and his companions were spared because they could catch fish
with nets, and they were so much prized on this ac-

count that a neighbouring chief made war on their
master to get possession of them, and being the
stronger, succeeded. In this way they spent thirteen years, being fought for and won by more than
twenty-five chiefs in that time, and in the course of
his wanderings the fisherman gained much information. He describes the country as very large, and,
as it were, a new world, the people very rude and
uncultivated. They go naked and suffer from the
cold, but have not the sense to clothe themselves
with skins. They live by hunting, but as they have
no metal, they use lances of wood sharpened at the
point and bound with strings of hide. They fight
fiercely, and afterwards eat the conquered. They
have chiefs, and laws which differ in the several
tribes. They grow more civilised towards the south-
west where the climate is milder, and they have
cities and temples to their idols, in which they
sacrifice men and afterwards eat them. In those
parts they have knowledge of gold and silver.

At last the fisherman determined, if possible, to
return to his country, and finally succeeded. He
worked his way to Drogio, where he stayed three
years, when some boats from Estotiland came to the
coast and received him on board as interpreter.
Finally, he returned to Frisland, and gave an account
of this important country to Sinclair.

This appears to have been, for the close of the
fourteenth century, a pretty good description of the
state of things in America as far down as Mexico.
It is evidently a *resumé* of the knowledge acquired

*

by the northmen in their expeditions to the west
and south-west. In addition to the information
gathered by the fisherman during his own long stay in
the country, he would, on his return to Greenland or
Iceland, hear much from those who kept up mercan-
tile connexion with America, to add to the store of
knowledge which he communicated to Sinclair.

One of the first achievements of the Greenland
colonists was the discovery of North America by
Lief, son of Erick the Red, in the year 1001. The
tracts of country there discovered were called Hellu-
land, *i.e.*, Slate Land, supposed to be Newfoundland : Markland, *i.e.*, Woodland, supposed to be
Nova Scotia : and Vinland or Vineland. There is
much uncertainty about the situation of the two
former, but the site of Vinland is less problematical.
One of the old writers says that on the shortest
day in Vinland the sun was above the horizon from
Dagmaal to Eikt, and as Dagmaal is known to have
meant half-past seven o'clock A.M., and Eikt half-
past four o'clock P.M., it follows that the length of
the day was nine hours, which gives the latitude of
forty-one degrees. This deduction is confirmed by
a curious coincidence. Adam of Bremen, writing in
the eleventh century, states on the authority of
Svein Estridson, King of Denmark, a nephew of
Canute the Great, that Vinland got its name from
the vine growing wild there, and for the same reason
the English re-discoverers gave the name of Martha's
Vineyard to the large island, close off the coast, in
latitude 41 degs. 23 min.

The old documents also mention a country called
Huitramannaland or Whiteman's Land, otherwise
Irland it Mikla or Great Ireland, supposed to include
North and South Carolina, Georgia and Florida. There
is a tradition among the Shawanese Indians, who
emigrated some years ago from Florida and settled
in Ohio, that Florida was inhabited by white people
who possessed iron instruments.   It is further recorded in the ancient MSS., that the Greenland Bishop
Erick went over to Vinland in the year 1121, and
that in 1266 a voyage of discovery to the arctic
regions of America was made under the auspices of
some clergymen of the Greenland Bishopric.   The
next recorded discovery was made by Adalbrand and
Thorwald Helgason, two Icelandic clergymen, in the
year 1285, the country found being supposed to be
Newfoundland.   The last record preserved in the old
Icelandic MSS. relates a voyage from Greenland to
Markland, performed by a crew of seventeen men in
the year 1347.   The account written by a contemporary nine years after the event, speaks of Markland
as a country still known and visited in those days,
and it was, until now, the latest document that
spoke of the maintenance of intercourse between
Greenland and America.   In the Zeno document,
however, we have the very latest evidence known
in literature of the continued existence of that intercourse down to the close of the fourteenth century,
a hundred years before the time of Columbus; for
although the valuable Codex Flateiensis, preserved
in Copenhagen, was completed at a period exactly

*

contemporary with that of the Zeni, it does not record such late details on this interesting subject. The descriptions of the old Icelandic MSS. sufficiently explain how Latin books, which had been taken over by the priests, should be found in the chief's possession. The woods of immense extent tell their own story. The importance of catching the codfish with nets, the description of the natives and their habits, the report of a country to the south rich in gold, are points in the Zeno narrative in harmony with our present knowledge and the testimony of the Icelandic records. Perhaps the most interesting, as showing the existence of Scandinavian people and customs in America at that period, is the statement of their making beer, which, as Zeno says, is "a kind of drink that northern people take as we do wine." Of the antiquity of beer-drinking in the north, we have proof from Sœmund the Learned, who in the eleventh century made that collection of poems known as the "Poetic Edda." In the "Lay of the dwarf Alvis" occurs the expression, "Ale it is called by men, but by the Æsir (gods) biorr." In the Copenhagen Museum are horns used of old by the Vikings for drinking beer. We have already had remarkable evidence that an inflated bombastic style may be used in the narration of a true story. When, therefore, in the description of a more remote country like America, we meet with such expressions as "the king's library" and "cities and temples," which might awaken misgivings as to the soundness of the story, we may revert to Zeno's account of the conquest of the Færoe Islands, and, recognizing the same inflated style as common to the stories, acknowledge that it would be unreasonable on that score to throw more doubt upon the one than upon the other.

It will be observed that in the Zeno narrative "Estotiland" is described as an *island* and "Drogio" as a *country*. The former was somewhat less than " Islanda," and as the description of it very fairly agrees with Newfoundland, the editor has here rendered the word Islanda "Iceland" and not "Shetland" as it is translated in those other parts of the narrative, where the latter was obviously meant. That he is justified in this selection of the larger of the two localities bearing the name of " Islanda" in the text to meet the comparison with Newfoundland as to size, will be seen by a reference to page 34 of the text, where it is shown that the book prepared by Antonio Zeno, but torn up by Nicolò Zeno, junior, contained descriptions of *both* Iceland and Shetland, although the former is left unnoticed in the text as we now have it, which was put together from the surviving letters of the ancient voyagers. Drogio, subject to such sophistications as the word may have undergone in its perilous transmission from the tongues of Indians *viâ* the northern fisherman's repetition, to the ear of the Venetian, and its subsequent transfer to paper, appears to have been a native name for an extensive tract of North America.

At length the expedition is organized for the

verification of the fisherman's statements and as the
story of its adventures is that part of the narrative
which has caused the greatest perplexity, it is here
given in full :—

" Our great preparations for the voyage to Estotiland were
begun in an unlucky hour, for three days before our departure the fisherman died, who was to have been our guide ;
nevertheless Zichmni would not give up the enterprise, but
in lieu of the fisherman, took some sailors that had come
out with him from the island. Steering westwards, we
discovered some islands subject to Frislanda, and passing
certain shoals, came to Ledovo, where we stayed seven
days to refresh ourselves and to furnish the fleet with
necessaries. Departing thence we arrived on the first
of July at the Island of Ilofe ; and as the wind was full
in our favour, we pushed on ; but not long after, when we
were on the open sea, there arose so great a storm that for
eight days we were continuously kept in toil, and driven we
knew not where, and a considerable number of the boats
were lost. At length, when the storm abated, we gathered
together the scattered boats, and sailing with a prosperous
wind, we discovered land on the west. Steering straight for
it, we reached a quiet and safe harbour, in which we saw an
infinite number of armed people, who came running furiously
down to the water side, prepared to defend the island.
Zichmni now caused his men to make signs of peace to
them, and they sent ten men to us who could speak ten
languages, but we could understand none of them, except
one that was from Shetland. He, being brought before our
prince, and asked what was the name of the island, and
what people inhabited it, and who was the governor, answered that the island was called Icaria, and that all the
kings that reigned there were called Icari, after the first
king, who as they said, was the son of Dædalus, King of
Scotland, who conquered that island, left his son there for
king, and gave them those laws that they retain to the

present time; that after this, when going to sail further, he
was drowned in a great tempest; and in memory of his
death that sea was called to this day the Icarian Sea, and
the kings of the island were called Icari; that they were
contented with the state which God had given them, and
would neither alter their laws nor admit any stranger.
They therefore requested our prince not to attempt to interfere with their laws, which they had received from that
king of worthy memory, and observed up to the present
time: that the attempt would lead to his own destruction,
for they were all prepared to die rather than relax in any
way the use of those laws. Nevertheless, that we might
not think that they altogether refused intercourse with
other men, they ended by saying that they would willingly
receive one of our people, and give him an honourable
position amongst them, if only for the sake of learning my
language and gaining information as to our customs, in the
same way as they had already received those other ten persons from ten different countries, who had come into their
island. To all this our prince made no reply, beyond en-
quiring where there was a good harbour, and making signs
that he intended to depart. Accordingly, sailing round
about the island, he put in with all his fleet in full sail, into
a harbour which he found on the eastern side. The
sailors went on shore to take in wood and water, which
they did as quickly as they could, for fear they might be
attacked by the islanders; and not without reason, for the
inhabitants made signals to their neighbours with fire and
smoke, and taking to their arms, the others coming to their
aid, they all came running down to the seaside upon our men,
with bows and arrows, so that many were slain and several
wounded. Although we made signs of peace to them,
it was of no use, for their rage increased more and more,
as though they were fighting for their own very existence.
Being thus compelled to depart, we sailed along in a great
circuit about the island, being always followed on the hill
tops and along the sea coasts by an infinite number of

h

armed men. At length, doubling the northern cape of the island, we came upon many shoals, amongst which we were for ten days in continual danger of losing our whole fleet; but fortunately all that while the weather was very fine. All the way till we came to the east cape, we saw the inhabitants still on the hill tops and by the sea coast, keeping with us, howling and shooting at us from a distance to show their animosity towards us. We therefore resolved to put into some safe harbour, and see if we might once again speak with the Shetlander, but we failed in our object; for the people, more like beasts than men, stood constantly prepared to beat us back if we should attempt to come on land. Wherefore Zichmni, seeing that he could do nothing, and that if he were to persevere in his attempt, the fleet would fall short of provisions, took his departure with a fair wind and sailed six days to the westwards: but the wind afterwards shifting to the south-west, and the sea becoming rough, we sailed four days with the wind aft, and at length discovered land."

Icaria has been supposed by many commentators to represent some part of America. Johann Reinhold Forster was the first to suggest that it meant Kerry, and the editor is convinced that he was right, although for reasons that Forster has not adduced. The name, the point of arrival, the conduct of the natives, and the movements of the fleet after leaving the island, all lead to this conclusion. The expression in the original " scoprimmo da Ponente terra" is susceptible of two meanings, either that they came upon an island " to the westward" or " upon its western side". But as, when repulsed by the natives, they sailed round about the island, and came into a harbour on its eastern side, it is manifest that the harbour which they first entered was on the west,

and in a position with which that of Kerry exactly
corresponds.

The signals by fire and smoke, the pursuit along
the hill tops and the howling of the strangers off
the coast are Irish all over. The sailing of the fleet
six days to the westward with a fair wind after leaving the north point of the island without seeing land,
is a fact which accords with the situation of Ireland,
but not with any part of America or any other
country otherwise answering the conditions.
Admiral Zahrtmann says :—

" As to the fabulous parts of the narrative, it is difficult
to select one passage in preference to another for refutation,
the whole being a tissue of fiction."

Now it happens that there is no room for selection in the matter, for there is only one piece of
fable in the whole story, and one cannot form a tissue
out of a single thread. That one piece of fable (it
must be understood that mere exaggerations of real
events are not fables) is the story of the Kings of
Icaria being called Icari after the first king, who was
the son of Dædalus, King of Scotland, in memory of
whose death by drowning that sea was called to this
day the Icarian Sea. The editor is strongly of opinion
that this excrescence on the narrative is the handy-
work of Nicolò Zeno, junior, and for the following
reason. The form of the name Icaria was a very
reasonable one for a southerner to give to the northern name of Kerry, but the northerners from whom
Zeno received it, would be little likely to tell him
such a story as that which we here have of Dædalus

and the Icarian Sea, which manifestly takes its origin from the form which the word had taken under the southerner's pen. On these grounds the editor suggests the reasonableness of the conclusion that Nicolò Zeno, junior, found in his ancestor's letter the name Icaria only, without the fable. But as, during the very time that intervened between his discovery of the letters when he was a boy and his publication of them, his fellow-citizen Bordone brought out two editions of his " Isolario," in which that well-known fable is told of the island of Nicaria (*olim* Icaria) in the Ægean Sea, it seems highly probable that this suggested to his mind the grafting of the story on the name which he had found transmitted by his ancestor under the same form.

After the fleet had sailed six days to the westward from Ireland, the wind shifted to the south-west and carried them to a harbour in Greenland. To this harbour and the headland near it they gave the name of Trin, and here Sinclair, being taken with the pureness of the atmosphere and the aspect of the country, conceived the idea of making a settlement, or, as Zeno calls it, " founding a city." As, however, his people were anxious to get home, he merely retained the row-boats and such of the men as were inclined to stay with him, and sent all the rest away under the command of Antonio. After twenty days' sail to the eastward and five to the south-east, Zeno found himself on Neome,— a locality which the editor need not trouble himself to speculate upon,—and in three days reached Frisland or Thorshavn, and so ends the story.

Now the question may be asked : *Cui bono* all this toil of analysis and research devoted to a document so unimportant in size and of such limited contents ? The facts may answer for themselves.

1. If the realities which have been here laid bare had been detected any time during the last three centuries and a quarter, so that the site of the lost East Colony of Greenland had been proved to demonstration instead of being a matter of opinion,[1] the Kings of Denmark would have been spared the necessity of sending out a great number of unsuccessful expeditions : and

2. A number of learned disquisitions by some of the most illustrious *literati* in Europe would have been rendered superfluous.

3. The Zeno document is now shown to be the *latest* in existence, as far as we know, giving details respecting the important lost East Colony of Greenland, which has been so anxiously sought for.

4. It is the *latest* document in existence, as far as we know, giving details respecting the European

---

[1] There can be no better proof of the correctness of this statement than the fact that while the true site was correctly believed in by Eggers in 1794, Captain Graah was sent out in 1828 to learn, if possible, whether the site were on the east or the west coast ; and even though he himself correctly believed in the true site, his pleas, on behalf of his convictions, were so inconclusive, that the learned author of " Iceland, Greenland, and the Faroe Islands" in 1840, after well weighing the arguments, says :—" For these reasons we are disposed to regard this point not only as still undecided, but one on which without more evidence it would be premature to come to any conclusion."

settlers in North America,—although a century before Columbus's great voyage across the Atlantic,—
and showing that they still survived at that period.

5. The honour of a distinguished man, whose only
faults as regards this ancient story, fruitful in mischief as they have been, were that he did not possess the geographical knowledge of to-day, and that
he indulged in the glowing fancies and diction of his
sunny country, has been vindicated : and

6. The book which has been declared to be "one
of the most puzzling in the whole circle of literature"
will henceforth be no puzzle at all.

GENEALOGICAL TREE OF THE ZENO FAMILY.

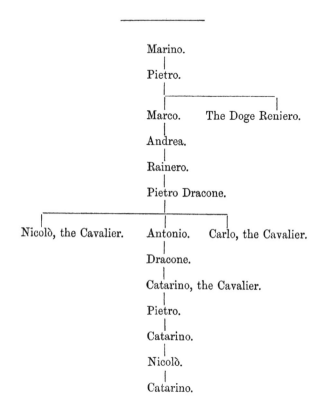

Marino.
|
Pietro.
|
Marco.   The Doge Reniero.
|
Andrea.
|
Rainero.
|
Pietro Dracone.
|
Nicolò, the Cavalier.   Antonio.   Carlo, the Cavalier.
|
Dracone.
|
Catarino, the Cavalier.
|
Pietro.
|
Catarino.
|
Nicolò.
|
Catarino.

THE DISCOVERY

Of the Iſlands of

FRISLANDA, ESLANDA, Engronelanda, Estotilanda, and Icaria:

Made by Two Brothers of the Zeno Family:

VIZ:

MESSIRE NICOLÒ, THE CHEVALIER,

and

MESSIRE ANTONIO.

With a Map of the said Islands.

The Discovery of the Islands of FRISLANDA, ESLANDA, ENGRONELANDA, ESTOTILANDA, and ICARIA : made by two Brothers of the ZENO Family, namely, MESSIRE NICOLÒ, the Chevalier, and MESSIRE ANTONIO.

With a Map of the said Islands.

IN the year of our Lord 1200, there was in the city of Venice a very famous gentleman named Messire Marino Zeno, who, for his great virtue and wisdom, was elected president over some of the republics of Italy; in the government of which he bore himself so discreetly, that his name was beloved and held in great respect, even by those who had never known him personally. Among other honourable actions of his, it is specially recorded that he set at rest some very serious civil disturbances which had arisen among the citizens of Verona, and from which were to be apprehended great provocations to war, had it not been for the interposition of his extreme activity and good advice.

Dello Scoprimento dell' Isole FRISLANDA, ESLANDA, ENGRONELANDA, ESTOTILANDA, & ICARIA, *fatto per due fratelli* ZENI, M. NICOLÒ *il Caualiere,* & M. ANTONIO. *Libro Vno, col disegno di dette Isole.*

NE' MILLE e dugento anni della nostra salute se molto famoso in Venetia M. Marin Zeno chiamato per la sua gran uirtù et destrezza d'ingegno podestà in alcune Republi. d'Italia, ne' gouerni delle quali si portò sempre così bene, che era amato, e grandemente riuerito il suo nome da quelli anco che non l'haueuano mai per presenza conosciuto ; e tra l' altre sue belle opere particolarmente si narra, che pacdficò certe graui discordie cittadinesche nate tra' Veronesi, dalle quali si aspettauano grandi motiui di guerra, se la sua estrema diligenza et buon consiglio non ui si fosse interposto. Di costui

B

This gentleman had a son named Messire Pietro, who was the father of the Doge Rinieri, who, dying without issue, left his property to Messire Andrea, the son of his brother Messire Marco. This Messire Andrea was Captain-General and Procurator, and held in the highest reputation for his many rare qualities. His son, Messire Rinieri, was an illustrious Senator, and several times Member of the Council. His son was Messire Pietro, Captain-General of the Christian Confederation against the Turks, and bore the name of Dragone because, on his shield, he bore a Dragon in lieu of a Manfrone, which he had borne previously. He was father of the great Messire Carlo, the famous Procurator and Captain-General against the Genoese in those perilous wars which were organised amongst nearly all the leading princes of Europe against our liberty and empire, and in which, by his great prowess, as Furius Camillus delivered Rome, so he delivered his country from an imminent risk which it ran of falling into the hands of the enemy. On this account he obtained the name of the Lion, which he bore painted on his shield as an enduring memorial of his deeds of

---

nacque M. Pietro, che fu padre del Duce Rinieri, ilqual Duce morendo senza lasciar di sè figliuoli fece suo herede M. Andrea, figliuolo di M. Marco suo fratello. Questo M. Andrea fu Capitan Generale, e Procuratore di grandissima riputatione per molte rare parti, ch' erano in lui ; ed fu suo figliuolo M. Rinieri, Senatore illustre, e piu uolte Consigliero ; di cui uscì M. Pietro, Capitan Generale della lega de' Christiani contra Turchi chiamato Dragone, perche nel suo scudo portò in cambio di un Manfrone, che haueua prima, un Dragone ; ilquale fu padre di M. Carlo il grande, chiarissimo Procuratore e Capitan Generale contra Genouesi in quelle pericolose guerre, che furono fatte mentre quasi tutti i maggiori Principi dell' Europa oppugnauano la nostra libertà e l' Imperio, nellequali per il suo ualore liberò, non altrimenti che un' altro Furio Camillo Roma, la sua patria da un' instante pericolo che correua di non diuenir preda de' suoi nimici ; onde perciò se ne acquistò il cognome di Leone, portandolo per eterna memoria delle sue prodezze nello

prowess. Messire Carlo had two brothers, Messire Nicolò
the Chevalier and Messire Antonio, the father of Messire
Dragone. This latter was the father of Messire Caterino,
father of Messire Pietro, whose son was another Messire
Caterino, who died last year, being the father of Nicolò,
now living.[1]

Now M. Nicolò, the Chevalier, being a man of great
courage, after the aforesaid Genoese war of Chioggia, which
gave our ancestors so much to do, conceived a very great desire to see the world and to travel and make himself acquainted
with the different customs and languages of mankind, so that
when occasion offered, he might be the better able to do service
to his country and gain for himself reputation and honour.
Wherefore having made and equipped a vessel from his own
resources, of which he possessed an abundance, he set forth
out of our seas, and passing the Strait of Gibraltar, sailed
some days on the ocean, steering always to the north, with
the object of seeing England and Flanders.[2] Being, how-

scudo dipinto. Di M. Carlo furono fratelli M. Nicolò il Caualiere,
e M. Antonio, padre di M. Dragone, delquale nacque M. Caterino,
che generò M. Pietro, di cui uscì un' altro M. Caterino, che morì
l' anno passato, padre di Nicolò, che ancor uiue. Or M. Nicolo il'
Caualiere, come huom di alto spirito, doppo la sudetta guerra Ge-
nouese di Chioggia, che diede tanto da far à i nostri maggiori, entrò
in grandissimo desiderio di ueder il mondo, e peregrinare, e farsi
capace di uarij costumi e di lingue de gli huomini, acciò che con le
occasioni poi potesse meglio far seruigio alla sua patria ed à se acquis-
tar fama, e honore. La onde fatta ed armata una naue delle sue
proprie ricchezze che amplissime haueua, uscì fuori de i nostri mari,
e passato lo stretto di Gibilterra nauigò alcuni dì per l' Oceano
sempre tenendosi uerso la Tramontana con animo di ueder l' Inghil-
terra, e la Fiandra, doue, assaltato in quel mare da una gran fortuna

---

[1] The editor of the present document.

[2] The Flanders voyage from Venice had been for a long series of
years prior to this period, a matter of frequent occurrence. The distinguished antiquary, Mr. Rawdon Brown, who has utilised his long

ever, attacked in those seas by a terrible storm, he was so
tossed about for the space of many days with the sea and
wind that he knew not where he was; and at length when
he discovered land, being quite unable to bear up against
the violence of the storm, he was cast on the Island of
Frislanda.[1] The crew, however, were saved, and most of
the goods that were in the ship. This was in the year
1380.[2] The inhabitants of the island came running in great
numbers with weapons to set upon Messire Nicolò and his
men, who being sorely fatigued with their struggles against
the storm, and not knowing in what part of the world they
were, were not able to make any resistance at all, much less
to defend themselves with the vigour necessary under such
dangerous circumstances ; and they would doubtless have

---

molti dì ando trasportato dalle onde e da' uenti senza sapere done
si fosse, quando finalmente scoprendo terra, ne potendo piu reggersi
contra quella fierissima burasca, ruppe nell'Isola Frislanda, saluandosi gli huomini e gran parte delle robbe, che erano sù la naue, e
questo fu l' anno mille e trecento ed ottanta. Qui concorrendo gli
isolani armati in gran numero assaltarono M. Nicolo ed i suoi, che
tutti trauagliati per la fortuna passata, non sapeuano in che mondo
si fossero, e per consequente non erano atti à far un picciolo insulto,
non che à difendersi gagliardamente, come il pericolo il portaua
contra tai nimici ; ed in ogni modo sarebbeno stati mal menati, se

---

residence in Venice by throwing so much light on Venetian history by
his researches, has given us in his " Archivio di Venezia con riguardo
speciale alla Storia Inglese", Venezia, 1865, p. 274, a list of the com-
manders of these expeditions from 1317 down to 1533.

    [1] Now known to be the Feroe Islands, as shown by the identity of
names laid down in the Frislanda of the Zeno Map, with those in the
Færoe group, e.g., Andefiord, Sueroe, Stromoe, and Monaco or the Monk.
Færoe, or Ferris Island of the Danes, becomes, in the mouth of an
Italian, who adds an " a" and accentuates the penultimate, " Frislanda."
Columbus, a hundred years later, carried away the same form of name
for the same group.

    [2] This date is certainly not correct ; say rather 1390. See remarks on
this subject in the Introduction.

been very badly dealt with, had it not fortunately happened
that a certain chieftain was near the spot with an armed
retinue. When he heard that a large vessel had just been
wrecked upon the island, he hastened his steps in the
direction of the noise and outcries that were being made
against our poor sailors, and driving away the natives,
addressed our people in Latin, and asked them who they
were and whence they came; and when he learned that they
came from Italy, and that they were men of the same
country,[1] he was exceedingly rejoiced. Wherefore promising
them all that they should receive no discourtesy, and as-
suring them that they were come into a place where they
should be well used and very welcome, he took them under
his protection, and pledged his honour for their safety. He
was a great lord, and possessed certain islands called Porlanda, lying not far from Frislanda to the south, being the
richest and most populous of all those parts. His name
was Zichmni,[2] and besides the said small islands, he was
Duke of Sorano, lying over against Scotland.

Of these north parts I have thought good to draw a copy

a buona uentura non faceua che casualmente si fosse trouato iui
uicino un Prencipe con gente armata, ilquale inteso che s'era rotta
pur all' hora una gran naue nell' Isola corse al romore ed alle
grida che si faceuano contra i nostri poueri marinai, e cacciati uia
quelli del paese, parlò in Latino, e dimandò che genti erano, e di
doue ueniuano, e saputo che ueniuano d'Italia, e che erano huomini
del medesimo paese fu preso di grandissima allegrezza. Onde, pro-
mettendo à ciascuno, che non riceuerebbeno alcun dispiacere, e che
erano uenuti in luogo nel quale sarebbeno benissimo trattati e
meglio ueduti, li tolse tutti sopra la sua fede. Era costui gran
Signore, e possedeua alcune Isole dette Porlanda, uicine à Frislanda
da mezzo giorno, le piu ricche e popolate di tutte quelle parti; e
si chiamaua Zichmni; ed oltra le dette picciole Isole signoreggiaua
fra terra la Duchea di Sorano, posta dalla banda uerso Scotia. Di
queste parti di Tramontana m'è paruto di trarne una copia dalla

[1] A blunder introduced by N. Zeno, Junior.
[2] Henry Sinclair, Earl of Orkney and Caithness.

of the sailing chart which I find that I have still amongst our family antiquities, and, although it is rotten with age, I have succeeded with it tolerably well; and to those who take pleasure in such things, it will serve to throw light on the comprehension of that which, without it, could not be so easily understood. Zichmni then, being such as I have described him, was a warlike, valiant man, and specially famous in naval exploits. Having the year before gained a victory over the King of Norway, who was lord of the island, he, being anxious to win renown by deeds of arms, had come with his men to attempt the conquest of Frislanda, which is an island somewhat larger than Ireland.[1] Whereupon, seeing that Messire Nicolò was a man of judgment, and very experienced in matters both naval and military, he gave him permission to go on board his fleet with all his men, and charged the captain to pay him all respect, and in all things to take advantage of his advice and experience.

---

carta da nauigare, che ancora mi truouo hauere tra le antiche nostre cose di casa; laquale, con tutto che sia marcia ed uecchia di molti anni, m' è riuscita assai bene; e posta dauanti gli occhi di che si diletta di queste cose, seruirà quasi per un lume à dargli intelligentia di quel che senz' essa non si potrebbe così ben sapere. Con tanto stato che s' è detto, Zichmni era bellicoso ed ualente e sopratutto famosissimo nelle cose di mare, e per hauer hauuto uittoria l' anno auanti del Re di Noruegia, che signoreggiaua l' Isola, com' huom, che desideraua con l' arme di farsi molto piu illustre che non era, con le sue genti era disceso per far l' impresa ed acquistarsi il paese di Frislanda, che è isola assai maggiore che Irlanda; onde, uedendo, che M. Nicolò era persona sensata, e nelle cose marinaresche e della guerra grandemente pratico, gli commisse che andasse sù l' armata con tutti i suoi, imponendo al Capitano che l'honorasse, ed in tutte le cose si ualesse del suo consiglio, come di quel che conosceua e

---

[1] From the Zeni's utter ignorance of Ireland, as shown in a subsequent part of the narrative, I have reason to suspect that the word rendered here "Irlanda", was in the original text "Islanda", as written elsewhere in the text for "Shetland".

This fleet of Zichmni consisted of thirteen vessels, whereof
two only were rowed with oars; the rest were small barks
and one ship. With these they sailed to the westwards, and
with little trouble gained possession of Ledovo[1] and Ilofe[2]
and other small islands in a gulf called Sudero, where in the
harbour of the country called Sanestol[3] they captured some
small barks laden with salt fish. Here they found Zichmni,
who came by land with his army, conquering all the country
as he went. They stayed here but a little while, and making
their course still westwards, they came to the other cape of
the gulf, and then turning again they fell in with certain
islands and lands which they brought into possession of
Zichmni. This sea through which they sailed, was in a
manner full of shoals and rocks; so that had Messire Nicolò
and the Venetian mariners not been their pilots, the whole
fleet, in the opinion of all that were in it, would have been
lost, so inexperienced were Zichmni's men in comparison

sapeua da se molto per lungo uso di nauigare e dell' arme. Questa
armata di Zichmni era di tredici legnì, due solamente da remo, il
resto nauigli ed una naue, con laquale nauigarono uerso Ponente,
e s'insignorirono con poca fatica di Ledouo, et di Ilofe, e di alcune
altre Isolette, uolgendosi in un golfo, chiamato Sudero, doue nel
porto della terra detta Sanestol, presero alcuni nauigli carichi di
pesce salato; e, trouato quì Zichmni, che con l' essercito di terra
era uenuto acquistando tutto il paese, poco ui si fermarono, perche
fatto uela pur per Ponente peruennero fin all' altro capo del golfo,
e girandosi di nuouo trouarono alcune isole e terre, che furono
tutte da lor ridotte in poter di Zichmni. Questo mare da lor
nauigato era in maniera pieno di seccagne e di scogli, che se non
fosse stato M. Nicolo il suo Piloto, ed i marinai Venetiani, tutta
quell' armata, per giudicio di quanti u' erano sù, si sarebbe perduta,
per la poca pratica, che haueuano quelli di Zichmni a comparatione

[1] Lille Dimon.
[2] Skuoe; the "S" of the MS. has doubtless been read as an "I".
[3] Sandöe.

with ours, who had been, one might say, born, trained up, and grown old in the art of navigation. Now the fleet having done as described, the captain, by the advice of Messire Nicolò, determined to go ashore at a place called Bondendon,[1] to learn what success Zichmni had had in his wars, and there to their great satisfaction they heard that he had fought a great battle and put to flight the army of the enemy; in consequence of which victory, ambassadors were sent from all parts of the island to yield the country up into his hands, taking down their ensigns in every town and village. They decided therefore to stay in that place to await his coming, taking it for granted that he would be there very shortly. On his arrival there were great demonstrations of joy, as well for the victory by land as for that by sea; on account of which the Venetians received from all such great honour and praise that there was no talk but of them, and of the great valour of Messire Nicolò. Whereupon the chieftain, who was a great lover of valiant men, and espe-

de i nostri, che nell' arte erano, si può dir, nati, cresciuti, ed inuecchiati. Or hauendo l'armata fatte quelle cose che si sono dette, il Capitano, col consiglio di M. Nicolò, uolle, che si facesse scala à una terra chiamata Bondendon per intender i successi della guerra di Zichmni, doue intese con suo molto piacere, che egli haueua fatto una gran battaglia, e haueua rotto l'essercito nimico; per laqual sua uittoria tutta l'isola gli mandaua Ambasciadori àfargli deditione, leuando le sue insegne per tutte le terre e castella; per il che gli parue di soprastar in quel luogo fin alla sua uenuta, dicendosi per fermo ch' egli tosto u' haueua da essere. Al suo arriuare si fecero grande dimostratione di allegrezza, così per la uittoria di terra, come per quella di mare, per laquale erano tanto honorati e celebrati da tutti i Venetiani, che non si sentiua d'altro parlare, che di loro, e del ualore di M. Nicolò. Onde il Prencipe, che era da si

[1] Norderdahl. The reader will bear in mind that these names are identified with those in the text, not by their written form, but by sound, for reasons given in the Introduction.

cially of those that were skilled in nautical matters, caused
Messire Nicolò to be brought before him, and after having
honoured him with many words of commendation, and
complimented his great zeal and skill, by which two
things he acknowledged himself to have received a very
great and inestimable benefit, viz. the preservation of his
fleet and the winning of so many places without any trouble
to himself, he conferred on him the honour of knight-
hood, and rewarded his men with very handsome presents.
Departing thence they went in triumphant manner towards
Frislanda,[1] the chief city of that island, on the south-east of
it, lying inside a bay in which there is such great abundance of fish that many ships are laden therewith to supply
Flanders, Brittany, England, Scotland, Norway and Denmark, and by this trade they gather great wealth.

The description thus far is taken from a letter sent by
Messire Nicolò to Messire Antonio, his brother, requesting
that he would find some vessel to bring him out to him.

---

amantissimo de' ualenti huomini, e di quelli specialmente che si
portauano bene nelle cose marinaresche, si fece uenir M. Nicolò, et
dopò hauerlo con molte honorate parole comendato et lodato la sua
grande industria e l' ingegno, dalle quali due cose diceua che rico-
nosceua un molto grande e rileuato benificio, come era quel di ha-
uergli saluata l' armata, ed acquistato senza alcuna sua fatica tanti
luoghi, lo fece caualiere, e honorati e donati di ricchissimi presenti
tutti i suoi, partì di quel luogo, ed à guisa di trionfanti per la uittoria hauuta, andò alla uolta di Frislanda, città principale dell' Isola,
posta dalla banda di leuante uerso ostro dentro un golfo, che molti
ne fà quell' isola, nelquale si prende pesce in tanta copia, che se ne
caricano molte naui, e se ne fornisce la Fiandra, la Bretagna, l'Ing-
hilterra, la Scotia, la Noruegia, e Danimarcha, e di quel ne cauano
grandissime ricchezze. Fin quì scriue M. Nicolò in una sua lettera
à M. Antonio suo fratello questi auisi, pregandolo, che con qualche

---

[1] Thorshavn. In medieval times it was a frequent custom to apply
the name of the country to the capital.

Whereupon, he having as great a desire as his brother to see the world and make acquaintance with various nations, and thereby make himself a great name, bought a ship, and, directing his course that way, after a long voyage in which he encountered many dangers, at length joined Messire Nicolò in safety, and was received by him with great gladness, not only as being his brother by blood, but also in courage.

Messire Antonio remained in Frislanda and dwelt there fourteen years, four years with Messire Nicolò, and ten years alone. Here they won such grace and favour with the prince that, to gratify M. Nicolò, and still more because he knew full well his value, he made him captain of his navy, and with much warlike preparation they went out to attack Estlanda [Shetland], which lies off the coast between Frislanda and Norway ; here they did much damage, but hearing that the King of Norway was coming against them with a great fleet to draw them off from this attack, they departed under such a terrible gale of wind, that they were driven upon certain shoals and a good many of their ships

---

naue lo uolesse andar à trouare. Perche egli, che non men era desideroso che si fosse il fratello, di ueder il mondo e praticar uarie genti, e perciò farsi illustre e grand' huomo, comprò una naue, e dirizzatosi à quel camino, doppo un lungo uiaggio ed uarij pericoli scorsi, giunse finalmente sano e saluo à M. Nicolò, che lo riceuette con grandissima allegrezza, e perche gli era fratello, e perche era fratello di ualore. Fermossi M. Antonio in Frislanda, e ci habitò quattordici anni, quattro con M. Nicolò, e dieci solo ; doue peruenuti in tanta gratia e fauor di quel Prencipe, che per gratificarnelo, ma piu, perche da se egli pur troppo il ualeua, fece Capitan della sua armata M. Nicolò, e con grande apparato di guerra si mossero all' impresa di Estlanda, che è sopra la costa tra Frislanda e Noruegia, doue fecero molti danni, ma inteso che il Re di Noruegia, con una grossa armata di naui, ueniua lor contra per distorle da quella guerra, si leuarono con una burasca si terribile, che cacciati in certe seccagine ruppero gran parte delle lor naui, saluandosi il

were wrecked. The remainder took shelter in Grislanda,[1] a
large island but uninhabited. The king of Norway's fleet
being caught in the same storm, was utterly wrecked and
lost in those seas. When Zichmni received tidings of this
from one of the enemy's ships that was driven by chance
upon Grislanda, he repaired his fleet, and perceiving that the
Shetlands lay not far off to the northward, determined to make
an attack upon Islanda[2] [or Shetland], which together with
the rest was subject to the king of Norway. Here, however,
he found the country so well fortified and defended, that his
fleet being but small and very ill-appointed both with
weapons and men, he was fain to give up that enterprise
without effecting anything, but removed his attack to the
other islands in those channels which are called Islande,
[or the Shetlands] which are seven in number, viz., Talas,

rimanente in *Grislanda*, isola grande, ma dishabitata. L' armata
del Re di Noruegia, anch' ella assaltata dalla medesima fortuna, si
ruppe et perdì tutta per quei pelaghi, di che hauuto auiso Zichmni
da un nauiglio de' nimici scorso per fortuna in Grislanda, hauendo
già racconcia la sua armata, ed uedendosi per la Tramontana uicino
alle Islande, si diliberò di assaltar Islanda, che medesimamente con
l' altre era sotto il Re di Noruegia; ma trouò il paese così ben
munito e guarnito di difesa, che ne fu ributtato per hauer poca
armata, e quella poca anco malissimo in ordine di arme e di genti.
Per laqual cosa si parti da quella impresa senza hauerui fatto nulla,
ed assaltò negli stessi canali l' altre Isole, dette Islande, che sono
sette, cioè *Talas, Broas, Iscant, Trans, Mimant, Dambere, e Bres;*

---

[1] Mainland in the Orkneys, which bore the name of Hross-ey,
or Gross-ey, *i.e.*, Great Island, which, under the pen of the Venetian,
becomes "Grislanda", by the same process that converts the Færoe
Islands, or Ferris Land, into "Frislanda".

[2] This name, which occurs again a few lines lower, is evidently a misreading for Eslanda, as in the title, and Estlanda on the preceding page,
which the names and the position indicated, *i.e.*, between the Feroe
Islands and Norway, show to mean the Shetland Islands. "Islanda" is
here the capital of the "Islande", or Shetland Islands, wherever that
may have been. Lerwick did not then exist.

*

Broas, Iscant, Trans, Mimant, Dambere, and Bres ;[1] and
having taken them all he built a fort in Bres, where he left
Messire Nicolò, with some small vessels and men and stores.
For his own part, thinking that he had done enough for the
present, he returned with those few ships that remained
to him, in all safety to Frislanda. Messire Nicolò being left
behind in Bres, determined the next season to make an ex-
cursion with the view of discovering land. Accordingly
he fitted out three small barks in the month of July, and
sailing towards the North arrived in Engroneland.[2] Here he
found a monastery of the order of Friars Preachers, and
a church dedicated to St. Thomas, hard by a hill which
vomited fire like Vesuvius and Etna.[3] There is a spring
of hot water there with which they heat both the
church of the monastery and the chambers of the Friars,
and the water comes up into the kitchen so boiling hot, that
they use no other fire to dress their victuals. They also put
their bread into brass pots without any water, and it is

---

e messo tutto in preda edificò una fortezza in Bres, nellaquale lasciò
M. Nicolò con alcuni nauigli, e genti, ed altre munitioni, ed egli
parendogli allhora di hauer fatto assai con quella poca armata, che
gli era rimasa ritornò à saluamento in Frislanda. M. Nicolò rimaso
in Bres si diliberò à tempo nuouo di uscir fuori, e scoprir terra;
onde armati tre nauigli non molto grandi del mese di Luglio fece
uela uerso tramontana, e giunse in Engroneland ; doue trouò un
monistero di frati dell' ordine de'Predicatori, ed una Chiesa dedicata
à San Tomaso appresso un monte, che butta fuoco come Vesuuio ed
Etna; et c' è una fontana di acqua affocata, con laquale nella chiesa del monistero, et nelle camere de' frati si fà' l' habitatione calda,
essendo nella cucina così bollente, che senza altro fuoco farui, si ser-
ueno al bisogno di quella, mettendo nelle pignatte di rame il pane

---

[1] It will be seen that the editor, Nicolò Zeno, Junior, in his misreading of the "Islande" of the text, has engrafted these islands or localities
on the east coast of Iceland, which island is also called Islanda. See
map.   [2] Greenland.
[3] On this volcano, see Introduction, p. lxxxv.

baked the same as if it were in a hot oven. They have
also small gardens covered over in the winter time, which
being watered with this water, are protected against the
effect of the snow and cold, which in those parts, being
situate far under the pole, are very severe, and by this means
they produce flowers and fruits and herbs of different
kinds, just as in other temperate countries in their seasons,
so that the rude and savage people of those parts, seeing
these supernatural effects, take those friars for Gods, and
bring them many presents, such as chickens, meat, and other
things, holding them as Lords in the greatest reverence and
respect. When the frost and snow are very great, these friars
heat their houses in the manner described, and by letting in
the water or opening the windows, they can in an instant
temper the heat and cold of an apartment at their pleasure.
In the buildings of the monastery they use no other material than that which is supplied to them by the fire; for
they take the burning stones that are cast out like cinders
from the fiery mouth of the hill, and when they are at their

senz' acqua, che si cuoce come in un forno ben riscaldato. Et ci sono
giardinetti, coperti di uerno, ilquali inafiati di quell' acqua si difen-
deno contra la neue et il freddo, che in quelle parti, per essere grandemente situate sotto il Polo, u' è asprissimo, onde ne nascono
fiori et frutti et herbe di uarie sorti, non altrimente che si facciano
ne' paesi temperati alle loro stagioni, per lequali cose le genti rozze
et saluatiche di quei luoghi, uedendo effeti sopra natura, tengono
quelli frati per Dei, et portano a lor polli, carne, et altre cose, et
come Signori li hanno tutti in grandissima riuerenza et rispetto.
Nel modo, adunque, che s' è detto, fanno questi frati, quando u' è
maggior il ghiaccio et la neue, la lor habitatione temperata, et possono in un' attimo riscaldar et raffreddar una stanza con far crescer
à certi termini piu l' acqua, et con aprir le finestre, et lasciarui en-
trar la freddura della stagione.   Nelle fabriche del monistero non
si seruono di altra materia che di quella stessa, che porta lor il
fuoco, perche tolgono le pietre ardenti, che à similitudine di fauille
escono dalla bocca dell' arsura del monte, allhora che sono piu in-

hottest they throw water on them and dissolve them, so that
they become an excellent white lime which is extremely tenacious, and when used in building never decays. These clinkers
when cold are very serviceable in place of stones for making
walls and arches ; for when once chilled they will never yield
or break unless they be cut with some iron tool, and the
arches built of them are so light that they need no strong
support, and are everlasting in their beauty and consistency.
By means of these great advantages these good friars have
constructed so many buildings and walls that it is a curiosity
to witness. The roofs of their houses are for the most part
made in the following manner : first, they raise up the wall
to its full height; they then make it incline inwards, by little
and little, in form of an arch, so that in the middle it forms
an excellent passage for the rain. But in those parts they are
not much threatened with rain, because the pole, as I have
said, is extremely cold, and when the first snow is fallen, it
does not thaw again for nine months, which is the duration
of their winter. They live on wild fowl and fish ; for, where

fiammate, et buttano lor sopra dell' acqua per laquale si apreno, et
fanno bitumo ò calcina bianchissima et molto tenace, che posta in
conserua non si guasta mai. Et le fauille medesime, estinte che
sono, seruen in luogo di pietre à far i muri et i uolti, perche, come
si raffreddano non si possono piu disfare ò rompre, se per auentura
non sono spezzate dal ferro; et i volti fatti di quelle sono in maniera
leggiero che non hanno bisogno di altro sostentacolo, et durano sempre
belli et in concio. Per queste tante commodità u' han fatto quei buon
padri tante habitationi et muraglie, che è uno stupore à uederle. Il piu
de' coperti che ui sono, si fanno in questo modo, che tirato il muro
fin alla sua altezza, lo uanno à poco à poco auanzando sopra il uolto,
tanto che nel mezzo forma un giusto piouer ; ma di pioggie non ci
si teme troppo in quelle parti, perche per essere il Polo, come s'è
detto, freddissimo, caduta la prima neue non si disfà piu, se non
passati i noui mesi dell' anno, che tanto tra lor dura il uerno.
Viueno di saluaticine e di pesci, percioche, doue entra l' acqua tis-

the warm water falls into the sea, there is a large and wide
harbour, which, from the heat of the boiling water, never
freezes all the winter, and the consequence is, that there is
such an attraction for sea-fowl and fish that they are caught
in unlimited quantity, and prove the support of a large
population in the neighbourhood, which thus finds abundant
occupation in building and in catching birds and fish, and
in a thousand other necessary occupations about the monastery.

Their houses are built about the hill on every side, round
in form, and twenty-five feet broad, and narrower and narrower towards the top, having at the summit a little hole,
through which the air and light come into the house; and
the ground below is so warm, that those within feel no cold
at all. Hither, in summer time, come many vessels from
the islands thereabout, and from the Cape above Norway,
and from Trondheim, and bring the Friars all sorts of com-
forts, taking in exchange fish, which they dry in the sun or
by freezing, andskins of different kinds of animals. By
this means they obtain wood for burning, and admirably

---

pida nel mare u' è il porto assai capace e grande, che per l' acqua
che bolle, di uerno non si congela mai. Là onde c' è tanto concorso
di uccelli marini, e di pesci, che ne prendeno un numero quasi infinito, col quale fanno le spese à un gran popolo iui uicino, che
tengono in continua opera, così nel tirar sù le fabriche, come nel
prender gli uccelli ed il pesce, e nel far mille altre cose che biso-
gnano al monistero. Le case di costoro sono intorno al monte tutte
rotonde, e larghe uenticinque piedi, e nell' alto si uanno stringendo
in maniera, che ui lasciano di sopra una picciola apritura, per doue
entra l' aere, che dà lume al luogo ; e la terra u' è così calda di
sotto, che dentro non ci sente alcun freddo. Quì di state uengono
molti nauigli dall ' Isole conuicine e dal capo di sopra Noruegia, e
dal Treadon, e portano à i frati tutte le cose che si possono disi-
derare, e le cambiano con lor per essi del pesce, che seccano all'aere
ed al freddo, et pelli di diuerse sorti di animali. Onde s' acquistano
legna d' abbruciare, e legnami eccellentemente lauorati, e grano, et

carved timber, and corn, and cloth for clothes. For all the countries round about them are only too glad to traffic with them for the two articles just mentioned; and thus, without any trouble or expense, they have all that they want. To this monastery resort Friars from Norway, Sweden, and other countries, but the greater part come from the Shetland Islands. There are continually in the harbour a number of vessels detained by the sea being frozen, and waiting for the next season to melt the ice. The fishermen's boats are made like a weaver's shuttle. They take the skins of fish, and fashion them with the bones of the self-same fish, and, sewing them together and doubling them over, they make them so sound and substantial that it is wonderful to see how, in bad weather, they will shut themselves close inside and expose themselves to the sea and the wind without the slightest fear of coming to mischief. If they happen to be driven on any rocks, they can stand a good many bumps without receiving any injury. In the bottom of the boats they have a kind of sleeve, which is tied fast in the middle, and when any water comes

---

panno da uestire ; conciosia che per il cambio delle due cose dette quasi tutti i conuicini disiderano di smaltir le mercatantie loro, ed essi senza a fatica e dispendio hanno ciò che uogliono. Ci concorreno in questo monistero frati di Noruegia, di Suetia, e di altri paesi, ma la maggior parte sono delle Islande. Et sempre in quel porto ci sono molti nauigli, che non possono partire per essere il mare aggiacciato ; ed aspettano il nuouo tempo, che lo disgele. Le barche de' pescatori si fanno come le nauicelle che usano le tessitori nel far la tela ; e tolte le pelle de' pesci le formano con alcuni ossi de' medesimi pesci, che le formano ; et cucite insieme, et poste in piu doppij, riescono sì buone e sicure, ch' è cosa certo miracolosa à sentire, nelle fortune ui si serrano dentro, et lasciano portarsi dall' onde, et da' uenti per il mare senza alcun timore ò di affogarsi ; e se danno in terra, stanno salde à molte percosse. Et hanno una manica nel fondo, che tengono legata nel mezzo, et quando entra acqua nel nauiglio, la prendeno nell' altra mità, e con due legni

into the boat, they put it into one half of the sleeve, then closing it above with two pieces of wood and opening the band underneath, they drive the water out; and this they do as often as they have occasion, without any trouble or danger whatever.

Moreover, the water of the monastery being sulphureous, is conveyed into the apartments of the principal friars in vessels of brass, or tin, or stone, so hot that it heats the place like a stove, and without carrying with it any stench or offensive odour whatever.

Besides this they have another means of conveying hot water by a conduit under the ground, so that it should not freeze. It is thus conducted into the middle of the court, where it falls into a large vessel of brass that stands in the middle of a boiling fountain. This is to heat their water for drinking and for watering their gardens. In this manner they derive from the hill every comfort that can be desired. These good friars devote the greatest attention to the cultivation of their gardens, and to the erection of handsome, but, above all, commodious buildings, nor are they wanting in ingenious and painstaking workmen for this purpose; for they are very liberal in their payments,

---

chiusi serrando di sopra, ed aprendo la legatura di sotto, cacciano l' acqua fuori ; et quante uolte occorre lor di far questo, lo fanno senza disconcio ò pericolo alcuno. L' acqua poi nel monistero per esser di zolfo li conduce nelle camere de' maggiori per certi uasi di rame, di stagno, ò di pietra, così calda, che come una stufa, riscalda benissimo la stanza senza che u' introduchi puzza, ò altro cattiuo odore. Oltra di questo, menano un' altra acqua uiua co' un muro sottoterra, acciò che non si agghiacci, fin nel mezzo della corte, doue cade in un gran uaso di rame, ilquale stà in mezzo di un fonte bollente, et cosi riscaldando l' acqua per il bere, et adacquar i giardini, hanno dal monte tutte le commodità, che si possono desiderar maggiori ; ne pongono in altro più cura quei buo' padri, che nel coltiuar bene i giardini, e nel far belle fabriche, et sopra tutto comode ; ne mancano lor in questo buoni ingegni, e huomini industriosi, perche pagano,

and in their gifts to those who bring them fruits and seeds they are unlimited in their generosity. The consequence is that workmen and masters in different handicrafts resort there in plenty, attracted by the handsome pay and good living.

Most of them speak the Latin language, and specially the superiors and principals of the monastery. This is all that is known of Greenland as described by Messire Nicolò, who gives also a special description of a river that he discovered, as may be seen in the map that I have drawn. At length Messire Nicolò, not being accustomed to such severe cold, fell ill, and a little while after returned to Frislanda, where he died.

Messire Antonio succeeded him in his wealth and honours ; but although he strove hard in various ways, and begged and prayed most earnestly, he could never obtain permission to return to his own country. For Zichmni, being a man of great enterprise and daring, had determined to make himself master of the sea. Accordingly, he proposed to avail himself of the services of Messire Antonio by sending

---

e donano largamente; ed uerso quelli, che portano frutti, e semenze sono senza fine liberali, e larghi nello spendere. Per il che u' è un grandissimo concorso di oure, e di maestramenti per esserci in quel luogo così buon quadagno, e miglior uiuere. Vsano il più d' essi la lingua Latina, e specialmente i superiori ed i grandi del monistero. Questo tanto si sà di Engroneland, dellaquale M. Nicolò descriue tutte le cose dette, e particolarmente la riuiera da lui discoperta, come nel disegno per me fatto si può uedere ; ed infine, non essendo egli uso à quelli freddi aspri, infermò, e poco dapoi ritornato in Frislanda morì.   Et M. Antonio successe nelle sue ricchezze, ed all' honore, ne, con tutto che tentasse molte uie, e pregasse e supplicasse assai, gli uenne mai fatto di ritornarsene à casa sua ; perche Zichmni, come huom di spirito e di ualore, si haueua al tutto messo in cuore di farsi padron del mare.   Onde, ualendosi di M. Antonio, uolle che con alcuni nauigli nauigasse uerso ponente, per essere state discoperte da quel lato da certi suoi

him out with a few small vessels to the westwards, because
in that direction some of his fishermen had discovered certain very rich and populous islands. This discovery Messire
Antonio, in a letter to his brother Messire Carlo, relates in
detail in the following manner, saving that we have changed
some old words and the antiquated style, but have left the
substance entire as it was.

Six and twenty years ago four fishing boats put out to
sea, and, encountering a heavy storm, were driven over the
sea in utter helplessness for many days ; when at length,
the tempest abating, they discovered an island called Estotiland,[1] lying to the westwards above one thousand miles
from Frislanda. One of the boats was wrecked, and six men
that were in it were taken by the inhabitants, and brought
into a fair and populous city, where the king[2] of the place
sent for many interpreters, but there were none could be
found that understood the language of the fishermen, except
one that spoke Latin,[3] and who had also been cast by chance

pescatori Isole ricchissime, e popolatissime ; laqual discoperta narra
M. Antonio in una sua lettera scritta à M. Carlo suo fratello così
puntalmente, mutate però alcune uoci antiche, e lo stile, e lasciata
star nel suo essere la materia. Si partirono uentisei anni fà quattro
nauigli di piscatori, i quali, assaltati da una gran fortuna molti
giorni andarono, come pur perduti per il mare, quando, finalmente
raddolcitosi il tempo, scoprirono una isola detta Estotilanda posta
in ponente, lontano da Frislanda piu di mille miglia, nellaquale si
ruppe un de' nauigli, e sei huomini, che u' erano sù, furono presi da
gli isolani, e condotti à una città bellissima e molto popolata, doue
il Re, che la signoreggiaua, fatti uenir molti interpreti, non ne trouò
mai alcuno che sapesse la lingua di quelli pescatori, se non un
Latino nella stessa isola per fortuna medesimamente capitato, il-

[1] Unquestionably in North America.
[2] Allowance must be made for Venetian exaggeration in the word
" city" and " king".
[3] Some acquaintance with Latin by Catholics in the North is not to
be wondered at ; we find it used by Sinclair, see p. 5.

upon the same island. On behalf of the king he asked
them who they were and where they came from; and
when he reported their answer, the king desired that they
should remain in the country. Accordingly, as they could
do no otherwise, they obeyed his commandment, and remained five years on the island, and learned the language.
One of them in particular visited different parts of the
island, and reports that it is a very rich country, abounding
in all good things. It is a little smaller than Iceland, but
more fertile; in the middle of it is a very high mountain,
in which rise four rivers which water the whole country. The inhabitants are very intelligent people, and possess
all the arts like ourselves; and it is believed that in time
past they have had intercourse with our people, for he said
that he saw Latin books in the king's library, which they
at this present time do not understand. They have their
own language and letters. They have all kinds of metals,
but especially they abound with gold. Their foreign intercourse is with Greenland, whence they import furs, brim-

---

quale dimandando lor da parte del Re che erano e di doue ueniuano,
raccolse il tutto, e lo riserì al Re, ilquale intese tutte queste cose,
uolle che si fermassero nel paese; perche essi facendo il suo co-
mandamento, per non si poter altro fare, stettero cinque anni nell'
isola ed appresero la lingua, et un di loro particolarmente fu in
diuersi parti dell' isola, e narra che è ricchissima ed abondant-
issima di tutti li beni del mondo, e che è poco minore di Islanda,
ma piu fertile, hauendo nel mezzo un monte altissimo, dalquale
nascono quattro fiumi, che la irrigano.   Quelli che l' habitano sono
ingeniosi, e hanno tutte le arti come noi; e credesi, che in altri
tempi hauessero commercio con i nostri, perche dice di hauer
ueduti libri Latini nella libreria del Re, che non uengono hora
da lor intesi; hanno lingua, e lettera separate, e cauano metall'
di ogni sorte, e sopra tutto abondano di oro, e le lor pratiche sono
in Engroneland, di doue traggono pellerecie, e zolfo, e pegola;

stone and pitch. He says that towards the south there is a
great and populous country, very rich in gold. They sow
corn and make beer, which is a kind of drink that northern
people take as we do wine. They have woods of immense
extent. They make their buildings with walls, and there
are many towns and villages. They make small boats and
sail them, but they have not the loadstone, nor do they
know the north by the compass. For this reason these
fishermen were held in great estimation, insomuch that the
king sent them with twelve boats to the southwards to a
country which they call Drogio; but in their voyage they
had such contrary weather that they were in fear for their
lives. Although, however, they escaped the one cruel death,
they fell into another of the cruellest; for they were taken
into the country and the greater number of them were eaten
by the savages, who are cannibals and consider human flesh
very savoury meat.

But as that fisherman and his remaining companions were
able to shew them the way of taking fish with nets, their lives
were saved. Every day he would go fishing in the sea and

---

ed uerso ostro narra, che u' è un gran paese molto ricco d'oro,
e popolato; seminano grano, e fanno la ceruosa, che è una sorte
di beuanda che usano i popoli settentrionali, come noi il uino;
hanno boschi d'immensa grandezza, e fabricano à muraglia, e
ci sono molte città, e castella; fanno nauigli e nauigano, ma non
hanno la calamità ne intendeno col bossolo la tramontana. Per
ilche questi pescatori furono in gran pregio, si che il Re li
spedì con dodici nauigli uerso ostro nel paese che essi chiamano Drogio; ma nel uiaggio hebbero così gran fortuna, che si
teneuano per perduti; tuttauia fuggiata una morte crudele,
diedero di petto in una crudelissima; perciò che presi nel paese
furono la piu parte da quelli feroci popoli mangiati, cibandosi
essi di carne humana che tengono per molto saporita uiuanda.
Ma, mostrando lor quel pescatore co' compagni il modo di prender
il pesce con le reti, scampò la uita; e pescando ogni dì in mare, e

in the fresh waters, and take great abundance of fish, which
he gave to the chiefs, and thereby grew into such favour
that he was very much liked and held in great considera-
tion by everybody.

As this man's fame spread through the surrounding
tribes, there was a neighbouring chief who was very anxious
to have him with him, and to see how he practised his
wonderful art of catching fish. With this object in view,
he made war on the other chief with whom the fisherman then was, and being more powerful and a better war-
rior, he at length overcame him, and so the fisherman was
sent over to him with the rest of his company. During the
space of thirteen years that he dwelt in those parts, he says
that he was sent in this manner to more than five-and-
twenty chiefs, for they were continually fighting amongst
themselves, this chief with that, and solely with the purpose
of having the fisherman to dwell with them; so that wan-
dering up and down the country without any fixed abode
in one place, he became acquainted with almost all those
parts. He says that it is a very great country, and, as it,
were, a new world; the people are very rude and unculti-

---

nelle acque dolci prendeua assai pesce, e lo donaua à i principali.
Onde se ne acquistò perciò tanta gratia, che era tenuto caro, ed
amato, e molto honorato da ciascuno.   Sparsasi la fama di costui
ne' conuicini popoli, entrò in tanto disiderio un signor uicino di
hauerlo appresso di se, ed ueder com' egli usaua quella sua mi-
rabil arte di prender il pesce, che mosse guerra à quell' altro
Signore, appresso ilquale egli si riparaua, e preualendo infine,
per essere piu potente ed armigero, gli fu mandato insieme con
gli altri; ed in tredeci anni che stette continuamente in quelle
parti, dice che fù mandato in quel modo à piu de uenticinque
Signori, mouendo sempre questo à quel guerra, e quel à quell'
altro, solamente per hauerlo appresso di se, e così errando andò
senza hauer mai ferma habitatione in un luogo lungo tempo, si
che conobbe et practicò quasi tutte quelle parti.   Et dice il paese
essere grandissimo, e quasi un nuouo mondo, ma gente roza e

vated, for they all go naked, and suffer cruelly from the cold, nor have they the sense to clothe themselves with the skins of the animals which they take in hunting. They have no kind of metal. They live by hunting, and carry lances of wood, sharpened at the point. They have bows, the strings of which are made of beasts' skins. They are very fierce, and have deadly fights amongst each other, and eat one another's flesh. They have chieftains and certain laws among themselves, but differing in the different tribes. The farther you go south-westwards, however, the more refinement you meet with, because the climate is more temperate, and accordingly there they have cities and temples dedicated to their idols, in which they sacrifice men and afterwards eat them. In those parts they have some knowledge and use of gold and silver.

Now this fisherman, after having dwelt so many years in these parts, made up his mind, if possible, to return home to his own country; but his companions despairing of ever seeing it again, gave him God's speed, and remained themselves where they were. Accordingly he bade them farewell, and made his escape through the woods in the direc-

---

priua di ogni bene, perche uanno nudi tutti, che patiscano freddi crudeli, ne sanno coprirsi delle pelli degli animali che prendeno in caccia; non hanno metallo di sorte alcuna, uiueno di cacciaggioni, e portano lancie di legno nella punta aguzze, ed archi, le corde de i quali sono di pelle di animali; sono popoli di gran ferocità, combatteno insieme mortalmente, e si mangiano l' un l'altro; hanno superiori, e certe leggi molto differenti tra di loro. Ma piu che si uà uerso garbino, ui si troua piu ciuiltà per l' aere temperato che ù è; di maniera, che ci sono città, tempij agli Idoli, ed ui sacrificano gli huomini e se li mangiano poi; hauendo in questa parte qualche intelligenza ed uso dell' oro e dell' argento. Or, sendo stato tanti anni questo pescatore in questi paesi, si deliberò di ritornar, se poteua, alla patria, ma i suoi compagni disperatosi di poterla piu riuedere, lo lasciarono partir à buon uiaggio, ed essi si rimasero là. Ond' egli, detto a lor à Dio, fuggiuia

tion of Drogio, where he was welcomed and very kindly
received by the chief of the place, who knew him and was
a great enemy of the neighbouring chieftain ; and so passing
from one chief to another, being the same with whom he
had been before, after a long time and with much toil he
at length reached Drogio, where he spent three years. Here
by good luck he heard from the natives that some boats had
arrived off the coast; and full of hope of being able to carry
out his intention, he went down to the seaside, and to his
great delight found that they had come from Estotiland. He
forthwith requested that they would take him with them,
which they did very willingly, and as he knew the language
of the country, which none of them could speak, they employed him as their interpreter.

He afterwards traded in their company to such good
purpose, that he became very rich, and fitting out a vessel
of his own, returned to Frislanda, and gave an account of
that most wealthy country to this nobleman [Zichmni]. The
sailors, from having had much experience in strange novel-
ties, give full credence to his statements. This nobleman

---

per i boschi uerso Drogio, e fu benissimo ueduto ed accarezzato
dal Signor uicino, che lo conosceua, e teneua grande nimistà con
l' altro ; e così andando di una in un' altra mano di quelli medesimi per liquali era passato, doppo molto tempo ed assai trauagli
e fatiche, peruenne finalmente in Drogio, nelquale habitò tre anni
continui, quando per sua buona uentura intese dà paesani, che
erano giunti alla marina alcuni nauigli, ond' egli entrato iu buona
speranza di far bene i fatti suoi, uenne al mare, e dimandato di
che paese erano, intese con suo gran piacere che erano di Estotilanda ; perche, hauendo egli pregato di essere leuato, fu uolentieri
riceuuto per hauer la lingua del paese, ne essendo altri che la
sapesse, lo usarono per lor interprete. Là onde egli frequentò poi
con lor quel uiaggio, si che diuenne molto ricco e fatto ed armato
un nauiglio del suo, se ne è ritornato in Frislanda, portando à
questo Signor la nuoua dello scoprimento di quel paese ricchissimo ;
ed à tutto se gli dà fede per i marinai, e molte cose nuoue che

is therefore resolved to send me forth with a fleet towards
those parts, and there are so many that desire to join in
the expedition on account of the novelty and strangeness
of the thing, that I think we shall be very strongly appointed, without any public expense at all. Such is the
tenor of the letter I referred to, which I [*i.e.* Nicolò Zeno,
Junior] have here detailed in order to throw light upon
another voyage which was made by Messire Antonio. He
set sail with a considerable number of vessels and men, but
had not the chief command, as he had expected to have,
for Zichmni went in his own person; and I have a letter
describing that enterprise, which is to the following effect:—

Our great preparations for the voyage to Estotiland were
begun in an unlucky hour, for exactly three days before our
departure the fisherman died who was to have been our guide;
nevertheless Zichmni would not give up the enterprise, but
in lieu of the deceased fisherman, took some sailors that had
come out with him from the island. Steering westwards, we
discovered some islands subject to Frislanda, and passing

---

approuano essere uero, quanto egli ha rapportato. Per laqual cosa
questo Signore s' è rissoluto di mandarmi con un' armata uerso
quelle parti, e tanti sono quelli che ui uogliono sù uenire, per la
nouità della cosa, che senza dispendio publico, penso che saremo
potentissimi. Questo si contiene nella lettera per me di sopra
allegata, e ho posto il suo tenor quì, à causa che s' intenda un' altro
uiaggio, che fece M. Antonio, ilquale partì con molte gente e
nauigli, non essendo però stato fatto Capitano, come da prima
haueua pensato, perche Zichmni in persona ui si uolle trouare, e
ho una lettera sopra questa impresa, che dice in questo modo.
L' apparato nostro grande per andar in Estotilanda fu incominciato
con mal augurio, perche tre dì à punto auanti la nostra partita,
morì il pescatore, che haueua da essere nostra guida ; tuttauia non
restò questo Signore di se quitar auanti il preso viaggio, prendendo
per guide in cambio del morto pescatore alcuni marinai che erano
tornati da quella isola con lui, et così si ponemmo à nauigar uerso
ponente, et scoprimo alcune isole soggette à Frislanda, et passate

certain shoals, came to Ledovo,[1] where we stayed seven
days to refresh ourselves and to furnish the fleet with
necessaries. Departing thence we arrived on the first
of July at the Island of Ilofe;[2] and as the wind was full
in our favour, we pushed on; but not long after, when we
were on the open sea, there arose so great a storm that for
eight days we were continuously kept in toil, and driven we
knew not where, and a considerable number of the boats
were lost. At length, when the storm abated, we gathered
together the scattered boats, and sailing with a prosperous
wind, we discovered land on the west.[3] Steering straight for
it, we reached a quiet and safe harbour, in which we saw an
infinite number of armed people, who came running furiously
down to the water side, prepared to defend the island.
Zichmni now caused his men to make signs of peace to
them, and they sent ten men to us who could speak ten

---

certe seccagne si fermammo à Ledouo, doue per sette dì fummo
per cagione di riposo, e di fornir l' armata delle cose necessarie.
Partiti di quì arriuiammo il primo di Luglio all' Isola di Ilofe, e
perche il uento faceua per noi senza punto fermarsi, passammo
auanti, ed ingolfatisi nel piu cupo pelago, non doppo molto ci
assaltò una fortuna cosi fiera, che per otto giorni continui ci tenne
in trauaglio, e balestrò senza saper, doue ci fossemo, perdendosi
gran parte de' nauigli; in fine tranquillitosi il tempo, si ragunarono
insieme i legni, che si erano smarriti da gli altri, e nauigando con
buon uento scoprimmo da ponente terra, perche dirizzate le uele à
quella uolta arriuammo in un porto quieto e sicuro, e uedemmo
un popolo quasi infinito posto in arme, ed in atto di ferire, essere
corso al lito per difesa dell' isola. La' onde Zichmni, facendo dar
à i suoi segno di pace gli isolani mandarono dieci huomini, che

---

[1] Lille Dimon.   [2] Skuoe.

[3] The Italian expression " da ponente" may mean "to the westward",
or " on its western side". That the latter is meant here is proved beyond question by the subsequent expression that they sailed round and
came to the eastern side of the island.

languages, but we could understand none of them, except one that was from Shetland. He, being brought before our prince, and asked what was the name of the island, and what people inhabited it, and who was the governor, answered that the island was called Icaria,[1] and that all the kings that reigned there were called Icari, after the first king, who as they said, was the son of Dædalus, King of Scotland, who conquered that island, left his son there for king, and gave them those laws that they retain to the present time; that after this, when going to sail further, he was drowned in a great tempest; and in memory of his death that sea was called to this day the Icarian Sea, and the kings of the island were called Icari; that they were contented with the state which God hath given them, and would neither alter their laws nor admit any stranger. They therefore requested our prince not to attempt to interfere with their laws, which they had received from that

---

sapeuano parlar in dieci linguaggi, ne fu inteso alcun di loro, fuor ch' un d' Islanda. Costui, sendo stato condotto dauanti il nostro Prencipe, e dimandato da lui come si chiamaua quell' isola, et quai genti l' habitauano, e chi la signoreggiaua, disse, che l' isola si chiamaua Icaria, e che tutti i Re, che haueano regnato in quella si chiamarono Icari dal primo Re, che ui fu, che dicono esser stato figliuolo di Dedalo Re di Scotia; ilquale, sendosi insignorito di quell' isola, ui lasciò per Re il figliuolo con le leggi che ancora gli isolani usano ; e doppo fatte queste cose, uolendo piu auanti nauigare, per una gran fortuna, che si leuò si sommerse; onde per la sua morte ancora chiamano quel mare Icareo, ed i Re dell' isola Icari, e perche si appagauano di quello stato che hauea lor dato Dio, ne uoleuano punto inouar costumi, non riceueuano alcun forestiero, e che perciò pregauano il nostro Prencipe, che non uolesse romper quelle leggi che haueano hauuto dalla felice

---

[1] Kerry. For detailed explanations respecting this and the story of the Icarian Sea, see the Introduction.

king of worthy memory, and observed up to the present
time : that the attempt would lead to his own destruction,
for they were all prepared to die rather than relax in any
way the use of those laws. Nevertheless, that we might
not think that they altogether refused intercourse with
other men, they ended by saying that they would willingly
receive one of our people, and give him an honourable
position amongst them, if only for the sake of learning my
language and gaining information as to our customs, in the
same way as they had already received those other ten persons from ten different countries, who had come into their
island. To all this our prince made no reply, beyond en-
quiring where there was a good harbour, and making signs
that he intended to depart. Accordingly, sailing round
about the island, he put in with all his fleet in full sail,
into a harbour which he found on the eastern side. The
sailors went on shore to take in wood and water, which
they did as quickly as they could, for fear they might be
attacked by the islanders ; and not without reason, for the

---

memoria di quel Re, ed osseruate fin allhora ; perche non lo potrebbe fare se non con manifesta sua ruina, essendo essi tutti
apparecchiati di lasciar anzi la uita, che di perder in alcun conto
l' uso di quelle ; nondimeno, accioche non paresse, che in tutto
rifiutassero il comercio de gli altri huomini, gli diceuano per con-
chiusione, che uolentieri hauerebbeno riceuuto un de' nostri, e
l' hauerebbeno tra loro fatto de' primi ; e questo sol per apprender
la lingua mia, e hauer relatione de' nostri costumi, cosi come haueuano già riceuuto quegli altri dieci d' altri diuersi dieci paesi, che
all' isola erano uenuti. A queste cose non rispose altro il nostro
Prencipe, se non che fatto ricercar doue ci era buon porto, fece
uista di leuarsi, e circondandol' isola si cacciò à piene ueile con
tutta l' armata in un porto mostratogli dalla banda di leuante, ne
quale fatto scala discesero i marinai à far legna et acqua con
quella prestezza che poterono maggiore, dubitando tuttauia di
non esser assaltate da gli isolani ; ne fu uano il timore, perche

inhabitants made signals to their neighbours with fire and smoke, and taking to their arms, the others coming to their aid, they all came running down to the seaside upon our men with bows and arrows, so that many were slain and several wounded. Although we made signs of peace to them, it was of no use, for their rage increased more and more, as though they were fighting for their own very existence. Being thus compelled to depart, we sailed along in a great circuit about the island, being always followed on the hill tops and along the sea coasts by an infinite number of armed men. At length, doubling the northern cape of the island, we came upon many shoals, amongst which we were for ten days in continual danger of losing our whole fleet; but fortunately all that while the weather was very fine. All the way till we came to the east cape, we saw the inhabitants still on the hill tops and by the sea coast, keeping with us, howling and shooting at us from a distance to show their animosity towards us. We therefore resolved to put into some safe harbour, and see if we might once again

---

quelli, che habitauano al d'intorno, facendo segno à gli altri con fuoco e con fummo, si misero tosto in arme, et soprauenendo gli altri, in tanto numero discesero al lito sopra di noi con arme e saette, che molti restarono morti, e feriti; ne ualeua, che si facesse segno di pace, che quasi che combattessero della somma di tutte le cose, s'incrudeliuano ogn' hor piu. Per laqual cosa ci fu forza a' leuare, e dalla lunga andar con un gran circuito girando intorno l'isola essendo sempre accompagnati per i monti e per le marine, da una moltitudine infinita di huomini armati; et cosi uoltando il capo dell' isola uerso tramontana trouarono grandissime seccagne, nellequali per dieci dì continui furono in molto pericolo di non perder l'armata; ma per buona nostra sorte fu sempre bellissimo tempo. Passando adunque auanti fin al capo di leuante, sempre uedeuano gli Isolani nelle sommità de monti, e' per i liti uenir con noi, et con grida et con saettarci dalla lunga dimostrar uerso di noi ogn' hor piu un medesimo animo nimico; perche si diliberammo di fermarsi in un porto sicuro, e ueder di parlar un'

speak with the Shetlander, but we failed in our object; for
the people, more like beasts than men, stood constantly
prepared to beat us back if we should attempt to come
on land.   Wherefore Zichmni, seeing that he could do
nothing, and that if he were to persevere in his attempt,
the fleet would fall short of provisions, took his departure
with a fair wind and sailed six days to the westwards : but
the wind afterwards shifting to the south-west, and the sea
becoming rough, we sailed four days with the wind aft, and
at length discovering land, as the sea ran high and we did
not know what country it was, were afraid at first to approach it; but by God's blessing, the wind lulled, and then
there came on a great calm.   Some of the crew then pulled
ashore, and soon returned to our great joy with news that
they had found an excellent country and a still better
harbour.   Upon this we brought our barks and our boats
to land, and on entering an excellent harbour, we saw in the
distance a great mountain that poured forth smoke, which

---

altra uolta con l' Islando ; ma non ci riuscì il disegno, percioche
quel popolo, poco men che bestiale in questo, stette continuamente
in arme con animo deliberato di combatterci, se hauessimo tentato
la discesa.   La onde Zichmni, uedendo di non poter far cosa alcuna,
e che s'egli fosse stato piu ostinato nel suo proposito, la uittouaglia
hauerebbe potuto mancar all' armata, si leuò con buon uento,
nauigando sei giorni per ponente ; ma uoltatosi il tempo à garbino,
ed ingagliarditosi perciò il mare, scorse l' armata quattro dì con
uento in poppa, et discoprendo finalmente terra con non picciolo
timore si appressammo à quella per essere il mar gonfio, et la terra
discoperta da noi non conosciuta ; nondimeno Dio ci aiutò, che
mancato il uento, ci pose in bonaccia ; onde alcuni de l'armata
andando à terra con i nauigli da remo, dopò non molto ritornarono,
e ci riferirono con sommo nostro piacere, che haueuano trouato
buonissimo paese, e miglior porto ; per laqual nuoua, rimorchiate
noi le naui, ed i nauigli, andammo à terra, ed entrati in un buon
porto uedemmo dalla lunga un gran monte, che gettaua fummo ;
ilche ci diede speranza, che nell' isola ci sarebbeno trouate genti ;

gave us good hope that we should find some inhabitants in
the island ; neither would Zichmni rest, although it was a
great way off, without sending a hundred soldiers to explore
the country, and bring an account of what sort of people
the inhabitants were. Meanwhile, they took in a store of
wood and water, and caught a considerable quantity of fish
and sea fowl. They also found such an abundance of birds'
eggs, that our men, who were half famished, ate of them to
repletion. Whilst we were at anchor here, the month of
June came in, and the air in the island was mild and pleasant beyond description ; but, as we saw nobody, we began
to suspect that this pleasant place was uninhabited. To
the harbour we gave the name of Trin, and the headland
which stretched out into the sea we called Capo de Trin.
After eight days the hundred soldiers returned, and brought
word that they had been through the island and up to the
mountain, and that the smoke was a natural thing proceeding from a great fire in the bottom of the hill, and that
there was a spring from which issued a certain matter like
pitch, which ran into the sea, and that thereabouts dwelt
great multitudes of people half wild, and living in caves.

---

ne con tutto che fosse assai lontano, restò Zichmni di mandar cento
buoni soldati, che riconoscessero il paese, e rapportassero quai
genti l' habitauano ; e fra tanto l' armata si fornì d' acqua e di
legna, e prese di molto pesce ed uccelli marini; ed ui si trouarono
tante uuoua di uccelli, che se ne satiarono le genti mezze affam-
mate. Mentre noi dimorauamo quì entrò il mese di Giugno, nel
qual tempo l' aere era nell' isola temperato e dolce piu che si possa
dire ; tuttauia, non ui si uedendo alcuno, entrammo in suspittione
che un sì bel luogo fusse dishabitato, e ponemo nome al porto, ed
alla punta, che usciua in mare Trin, e Capo di Trin. I cento soldati
andati doppo otto dì ritornarono, e riferirono essere stati per
l' isola ed al monte, e che quel fummo nasceua, perche dimostraua,
che nel suo fondo u' era gran fuoco, e che era una fontana, dalla-
quale nasceua una certa materia come pegola, che correua al mare;
e che u' habitauano molte genti intorno mezzo seluatiche riparan-

They were of small stature, and very timid; for as soon as they saw our people they fled. into their holes. They reported also that there was a large river, and a very good and safe harbour. When Zichmni heard this, and noticed that the place had a wholesome and pure atmosphere, a fertile soil, good rivers, and so many other conveniences, he conceived the idea of fixing his abode there, and founding a city. But his people, having passed through a voyage so full of fatigues, began to murmur, and to say that they wished to return to their own homes, for that the winter was not far off, and if they allowed it once to set in, they would not be able to get away before the following summer. He therefore retained only the row boats and such of the people as were willing to stay with him, and sent all the rest away in the ships, appointing me, against my will, to be their captain. Having no choice, therefore, I departed, and sailed twenty days to the eastwards without sight of any land; then, turning my course towards the south-east, in five days I lighted on land, and found myself on the island of Neome, and, knowing the country, I perceived I was past Iceland;

dosi nelle cauerne di picciola statura e molte paurose, perche subito che ci uidero fuggirono nelle cauerne; e che u' era un gran fiume, ed un porto buono e sicuro. Di che informato Zichmni, uedendo il luogo con aere salubre e sottile, e con miglior terreno, e fiumi, e tante altre particolarità entrò in pensiero di farlo habitare, e di fabricarui una città; quando la sua gente, stanca hoggi mai di un viaggio così pien di trauagli, cominciò a tumultuare ed à dire che uoleuano ritornar à casa, perche il uerno era uicino, e che, se lo lasciauano entrare, non s' hauerebbeno poi potuto più partire, se non la state che ueniua. Per laqual cosa egli ritenuti solamente i nauigli da remo e quelli che ui uoleuano restare, rimandò gli altri in dietro tutti con le naui, ed uolle che contra mia uoglia io fossi lor Capitano. Partitomi adunque, poi che altro non si poteua fare, senza mai ueder terra nauigai uerso leuante uenti giorni continui; uoltatomi poi uerso siloco doppo cinque dì scopersi terra, trouandomi arriuado nell' Isola Neome, e conosciuto

and as the inhabitants were subject to Zichmni, I took in
fresh stores, and sailed with a fair wind in three days to
Frislanda, where the people, who thought they had lost
their prince, in consequence of his long absence on the
voyage we had made, received us with a hearty welcome.
What happened subsequently to the contents of this letter
I[1] know not beyond what I gather from conjecture from
a piece of another letter, which is to the effect: That
Zichmni settled down in the harbour of his newly-discovered
island, and explored the whole of the country with great
diligence, as well as the coasts on both sides of Greenland, because I find this particularly described in the sea
charts ; but the description is lost. The beginning of the
letter runs thus :—

Concerning those things that you desire to know of me,
as to the people and their habits, the animals, and the countries adjoining, I have written about it all in a separate

il paese, mi accorsi di hauer passato Islanda ; perche presi rinfres-
camenti da gli isolani, che erano sotto l' Imperio di Zichmni,
nauigai con buon uento in tre dì in Frislanda ; doue il popolo, che
credeua di hauer perduto il suo Prencipe per si lunga dimora che nel
uiaggio haueuamo fatto, ci raccolse con segni di grandissima allegrezza.

Doppo questa lettera non trouo altro, se non che per congettura
giudico, come posso trar da un' altro capo di un' altra lettera, che
porrò qui di sotto, che Zichmni fece una terra nel porto dell' isola da
lui nouellamente discoperta, e che dato si meglio à cercar il paese la
discoprì tutta, insieme con le riuiere dell' una ed altra parte di
Engroneland ; perche la ueggo particolarmente discretta nella carta
da nauigare ; nondimeno la narratione è perduta. Il capo della
lettera dice così. Quanto à sapere le cose, che mi ricercate de' costumi de gli huomini, de gli animali, e de' paesi conuicini, io ho

[1] The reader will perceive that this paragraph which, in common with
that which precedes and that which follows it, is written in the first
person, is indited by the Editor, Nicolò Zeno, Junior ; while the other
two are from the letters of his ancestor, Antonio.

D

book, which, please God, I shall bring with me. In it I
have described the country, the monstrous fishes, the customs and laws of Frislanda, of Iceland, of Shetland, the king-
dom of Norway, Estotiland, and Drogio; and, lastly, I have
written the life of my brother, the Chevalier, Messire Nicolò,
with the discovery which he made, and all about Greenland.
I have also written the life and exploits of Zichmni, a prince
as worthy of immortal memory as any that ever lived for
his great bravery and remarkable goodness. In it I have
described the discovery of Greenland on both sides, and
the city that he founded. But of this I will say no more in
this letter, and hope to be with you very shortly, and to
satisfy your curiosity on other subjects by word of mouth.

All these letters were written by Messire Antonio to
Messire Carlo his brother; and I[1] am grieved that the book
and many other writings on these subjects have, I don't
know how, come sadly to ruin ; for, being but a child when

---

fatto di tutto un libro distinto, che piacendo à Dio porterò con
meco ; nelquale ho descritto il paese, i pesci mostruosi, i costumi,
le leggi di Frislanda, di Islanda, di Estlanda, del Regno di Noruegia, di Estotilanda, di Drogio, ed infine la uita di Nicolò il Caualiere,
nostro fratello, con la discoperta da lui fatta, e le cose di Grolanda.
Ho anco scritto la uita e le impresse di Zichmni, Prencipe certo
degno di memoria immortale quando mai altro sià stato al mondo
per il suo molto ualore, e molta bontà, nellaquale si legge lo scoprimento di Engrouiland da tutte due le parti, e la città edificata
da lui. Però non ui dirò altro in questa lettera, sperando tosto di
essere con uoi, e di sodisfarui di molte altre cose con la uiua uoce.
Tutte queste lettere furono scritte da M. Antonio à M. Carlo suo
fratello, e mi dolgo che il libro, e molte altre scritture pur in
questo medesimo proposito siano andati, non sò come, miseramente
di male ; perche io ancor fanciullo, e peruenutomi alle mani, ne

---

[1] Here, again, the reader will perceive that though the language runs
on in the first person, there is a transition from the text of the old writer,
Antonio's, letter, to the current explanatory remarks of his descendant,
the Editor, Nicolò Zeno, Junior.

they fell into my hands, I, not knowing what they were, tore them in pieces, as children will do, and sent them all to ruin : a circumstance which I cannot now recall without the greatest sorrow. Nevertheless, in order that such an important memorial should not be lost, I have put the whole in order, as well as I could, in the above narrative ; so that the present age may, more than its predecessors have done, in some measure derive pleasure from the great discoveries made in those parts where they were least expected ; for it is an age that takes a great interest in new narratives and in the discoveries which have been made in countries hitherto unknown, by the high courage and great energy of our ancestors.

FINIS.

---

sapendo ciò che fossero, come fanno i fanciulli, le squarciai e mandei tutte à male, ilche non posso, se non con grandissimo dolore, ricordarmi hora. Pur, perche non si perda una si bella memoria di cose, quel che ho potuto hauere in detta materia, ho posto per ordine nella narratione di sopra ; acciò che se ne sodisfaccia in qualche parte questa età, che più che alcun' altra mai passata, mercè di tanti scoprimenti di nuoue terre fatte in quelle parti doue à punto meno si pensaua che ui fossero, è studiosissima delle narrationi nuoue, e delle discoperte de' paesi non conosciuti fatte dal grande animo e grande industria de i nostri maggiori.

IL FINE.

APPENDIX.

DESCRIPTION OF GREENLAND
IN THE FOURTEENTH CENTURY,

BY

IVAR BARDSEN.

DESCRIPTION OF GREENLAND

IN THE FOURTEENTH CENTURY,

BY

IVAR BARDSEN.

It is reported by men of experience, natives of Greenland, and recently come from thence, that from Stad in Norway to Horn on the east coast of Iceland, is seven days sailing due west. From Snaefjeldsnaes in Iceland, from which point the passage to Greenland is the shortest, the course is two days and two nights due west, and there you will find Gunnbjorn's Rocks midway between Greenland and Iceland. In old times this was the customary route, but now the ice that has been brought down from the northern

---

Descriptio Grœnlandiæ auctore IVARE BARDI *filio.*

Saa sigger vise Mend, som føde ehre udi Grönnland, och sist komne aff Grönnland, att norden aff Stad udi Norge er VII Dagge Seyling rett udi Vester thill Horns, som ligger østen paa Island.

Item fraa Snefelsnes aff Island, som er stackist till Grönnland, 2 Dage och thou Netters Seyling, rett i Vester att zeylle, och der ligger Gunbjornsschier rett paa Mittveyen emellum Grönland och Island. Thette vaar gammell Seylling ; en nu er kommen Is udaff landnorden

Sic dicunt viri periti, qui in Grönlandia nati sunt et nuperrime ex Grönlandia advenerunt, ex boreali parte Stadi Norvegiæ septem dierum navigationem esse, recta versus occidentem, ad Hornum, in orientali Islandiæ littore situm. Ab Snefelsneso Islandiæ, quâ brevissimus in Gronlandiam trajectus est, duorum dierum et duarum noctium spatio navigandum est recto cursu versus occidentem ; ibique Gunnbjörnis scopulos invenies, inter Grönlandiam et Islandiam medio situ interjacentes. Hic cursus antiquitûs frequentabatur, nunc vero glacies ex recessu

recess of the ocean, has adhered so closely to the above-named rocks that no one can hold the ancient course without placing his life in danger. From Long-naes, the northernmost point in Iceland near the above-named Horn, is two days' and two nights' sail to Svalbard in Havsbotnis. They who wish to sail direct from Bergen in Norway, to Greenland without touching Iceland, must sail due west, until they find themselves twelve nautical miles south of Reykianaes, a promontory on the south coast of Iceland, and by continuing this coast to the westward they will come to the high land of Greenland, called

---

Botnen saa ner forschreffne Scher, att ingen kan uden Liffs Fare deun gamble Leed seyle, som hereffter hörres.

Item fraa Langenes, som ligger nordist paa Island ved forchreffne Horn, ehr II Dagges och II Netters Seyling till Svalbarde i Haffsbotnen.

Item de som seyle ville udaff Bergen rettledes till Grönnland, och komme iche till Island, da schulle de zeylle rett udi Vester, saa lenge de komme synden ved Island till Reychenes, och da schulle de vere XII Uger Sœes sønder i Haffed aff forchreffne Reychens, och saa med forchreffne vesterlede schall hand komme under, det höye Land udi Grönnland, som heder

oceani euroaquilonari delata scopulos ante memoratos tam prope attigit, ut nemo sine vitæ discrimine antiquum cursum tenere possit, quemadmodum infra dicetur.

Ab Longoneso, quod in Islandia, maxime septentrionem versus, juxta Hornum supra memoratum situm est, duorum dierum et duarum noctium navigatio est ad Svalbardum in Havsbotnis.

Qui Bergis recto cursu in Grönlandiam navigare, neque ad Islandiam appellere volunt, his recta versus occidentem navigandum est, donec venerint e regione Reykenesi, australis Islandiæ promontorii, ita ut duodecim milliaria maritima ab australi parte hujus promontorii absint, atque ita cursu, ut modo dictum, occidentum versus continuato, ad altam Grönlandiæ terram, quæ Hvarvum dicitur,

Hvarf. A day before you sight the said Hvarf, you ought to see another lofty mountain called Hvidserk; under the two said mountains named, Hvarf and Hvidserk, is a headland named Herjulfsnaes, near which is a harbour named Sandhavn, which is frequented by Norwegians and merchants. Any one sailing from Iceland [to Greenland] must shape his course from Snaefjeldsnaes in Iceland, which is twelve nautical miles further to the west than the abovementioned Reykianaes, and for a day and a night he will sail due west, but must then steer south-west to avoid the ice that adheres to Gunnbjorn's Skerries. After that he must sail one day and one night to the north-west, which will bring him straight to that highland of Greenland

Hvarf; een Dag tillforn, för mand kand see forschreffne Hvarf, schall hand se ett andet höitt Bergh, som heder Hvidserk; en under forschreffne thou Fjelld, som Hvarf heder och Hvidserk, ligger edt Nes, som heder Herjulfsnes, och derved ligger en Haffn, som hedder Sand, almindelig Haffn for Normænd och Kjøbmænd.

Item seyller mand udaff Island, da schall hand thagge sinn Kaes fraa Snefelsnes, som ligger een Thølldt Søes vester lenger paa Island end forschreffne Reychenes, och seylle da rett udi vester een Dagh och een Natt, en stevne siden i Sudvest, att fly forschreffne Is, som ligger ved Gunbiörnsscher, och siden een Dag och een Natt rett i Nordvest; och saa kommer hand rettledis under forschreffne

pervenient. Pridie quam antedictum Hvarvum conspexeris, alium excelsum montem, qui Hvidserkus appellatur, conspexisse debes. Sed sub ante dictis duobus montibus, qui dicuntur Hvarvum et Hvidserkus, promontorium jacet, Herjulvsnesum dictum, cui adjacet portus nomine Sandus, Norvegis ac mercatoribus communis.

Si quis ab Islandia navigat, ab Snefelsneso, qui duodecim milliaribus maritimis longius versus occidentem in Islandia jacet quam antedictum Reykenesum, cursum dirigere debet, et recta versus occidentem navigare uno die et una nocte, sed postea in libanotum cursum dirigere, ut glaciem scopulis Gunnbjörnis adhærentem evitet, deindeque uno die et una nocte recta versus japygem; sic recto cursu ad altam illam terram Grön-

named Hvarf, under which lie the above-named Herjulfsnaes and Sandhavn. The inhabited part of Greenland lying the most to the east, and next to Hjerulfsnaes on the east, is called Skage Fjord, which is a very much frequented place. At a great distance eastward from Skage Fjord, is a harbour called Bere Fjord, quite uninhabited. Across its mouth are long reefs of sand, so that no large ships can enter except at high tide, but when high tide sets in, an immense number of whales come into the gulf, and at no time is there any lack of abundance of fish in Bere Fjord. The whale fishery is public in this gulf, but not without the bishop's consent, for the fjord belongs to the cathedral church. Inside it there is a great whirl-

---

höye Land Hvarf i Grönnland, som forschreffne Herjulfsnes och Sandhaffn ligger under.

Item den østerste Bygd, som er udi Grönnland, ligger rett for Østen ved Herjulfsnes, och hedder Skagefjord; det er en stor Bygd. Item langt øster aff Skagefjord ligger en Fjord, och er iche bygt, som hedder Berefjord, och framb i Fjorden ligger ett langt Reff thvertt for Indgangen, saa at ingen store Schiff maa der indkomme, uden daa stoer Ström ehr; och tha nar stoer Ström løber, løbe der utallige Hvalle; i den samme Berefjord vantter aldrig Fische; udi den samme Fjord er allmindelig Hvaellfischeri, och dog mett Biscopens Loff, thi Fjorden ligger till Dombkierchen. Och udi

landiæ, Hvarvum, sub qua antedictum Herjulvsnesum et Sandhavnia sita sunt, perveniet. Tractus habitatus Grönlandiæ, maxime in orientem vergens, Herjulvsneso proximus ab oriente est Skagefjordus dictus, qui locus magnopere frequentatus est.

Longo ab Skagefjordo spatio versus orientem sinus est, nullis coloniis frequentatus, dictus Berefjordus, in cujus sinus ostio longæ syrtes in transversum patent, ut nulla majora navigia, nisi maximis æstibus, ingredi possint, maximo vero æstu incidente, immensa cetorum multitudo in sinum incurrit. Eodem Berefjordo copia piscium nunquam deest. Est in eodem sinu publica cetorum captura, tamen cum veniâ episcopi, nam sinus templo cathedrali proprius

pool, called the Whale's Whirlpool, into which the whales
enter when the tide runs out. Still further eastward from
Bere Fjord is another fjord, called Ollum-lengri, or "Longest
of all"; at its mouth it is narrow, but further in very wide.
Its length is so great that no one knows the end of it. It is
tideless, has a great number of small islands in it, and there
is a great abundance of birds and birds' eggs in it. On
both sides extend great plains, covered with green grass
wherever you go. Further east, up to the Ice mountain, is
a harbour called Finnsbuda, so named because in Saint
Olaus's time a vessel was wrecked there, in which, as the
story still goes in Greenland, one of Saint Olaus's min-
isters, with some others, was drowned; those who sur-

---

den Fjord ligger en stoer Høøll,
enn Hvaells-Høøl, och første
søenn gaar ud, daa løber all
Hvallfischen i thend samme
Høøll.

Item øster lenger fraa forschreffne Berefjord ligger enn Fjord,
som hedder Ollumlengri; hand
er móó udenfore och megett
bredere inden till; hand er saa
lang, att ingen ved Ende paa
hannem; hand haffver ingen
Ström i sig; hand er fulld med
smaa Hollme; der ehr noch
Fugle och Egh; der er slett
Land paa bade Sider, voxitt
med grönntt gres, saa langt som
nogen Mand der farer. Item
øster lenger, till Issbergen ligger
en Haffn, som hedder Finsbuder,
saa kallit, fordi att i St. Olluffs
Thid brød der ett Schiff, som
allmindig Røgte ganger end udi

est. In hoc sinu ingens est
vorago, cetorum dicta, in quam
ceti recedente æstu incurrunt.
Longius orientem versus ab
antedicto Berefjordo alius sinus
est, dictus Omnium-longissimus,
qui ab angusto aditu in vastius
spatium diffusus, tantum in
longitudinem patet, ut finem
ejus nemo noverit. Hic nullo
æstu agitatus, parvis insulis
scatet, magna avium et ovorum
abundantia; utrinque planities
campestris, quæ quantum pro-
grediare viridi gramine vestita
est.

Longius versus orientem ad
molem usque glacialem portus
est, dictus Finnsbudæ, ita dictæ
quod jam ætate Olavi Sancti
navis aliqua eo loco naufragium
fecit, qua navi vectum Sancti
Olavi ministrum cum nonnullis
aliis mari periisse vulgata adhuc

vived buried those that perished, and over their graves set
great stone crosses, which are standing at the present day.
In going further eastward towards the Ice mountain, one
comes to a large island called Korsöe, in which is a general
hunting ground of white bears, but not without permission
of the bishop, for the island belongs to the cathedral church.
From this point eastward, nothing presents itself to the eye
but ice and snow, either by land or water.
But to return to the subject we have above referred to,
with respect to the Greenland colonies. We have already
pointed out in speaking of the provinces of Greenland, that
Skagefjord, which lies to the east of Herjulfsnaes, is the
easternmost of the inhabited districts in Greenland. West-

Dag udi Grönland, at oppaa
det Schib var St. Olluffs Smas-
vend, och hand druchnede der
med de andre, och de som daa
effterleffde, groffve der nedr de
Døde, och reste der op store
Stenkors paa de Dødes Graffver,
och de stande enn udi Dagh.
Item øster lenger till Isbjergen
ligger en stor Øe, som hedder
Kaarsøøe. ThererallminnigJact-
vedtschaff effter hvide Björne,
och da med Bispens Orloff, thi
den Øe høerer Dombkierchen
till. Da er gindted øster lenger,
da mand kand see, uden Is och
Sne bade till Land och vand.
Item at komme till den Ma-
teriem, som föere røertt er om
Bygder paa Grönnland, som sagt
var om Bygder paa Grönnland,
at Skagefjord er østerst Bygd
paa Grönnland østen Herjulfsnes.

in Grönlandia fama refert, super-
stites vero mortuos sepilivisse
et super horum sepulcris cruces
magnas lapideas erexisse, quæ
hodieque ibi stant. Longius
orientem versus proficiscenti ad
molem glacialem obvia est
magna insula, dicta Korsöa,
ubi publica est alborum ursorum
captura, permissu tamen episcopi, quod ea insula peculium
est ædis cathedralis. Longius
versus orientem nihil præter
glaciem et nivem terrâ marive
conspici datur.
Ut ad rem, quam supra atti-
gimus, de coloniis Grönlandiæ,
redeamus, jam supra provincia-
rum Grönlandiæ mentionem
facientes indicavimus, Skagefjor-
dum, ab orientali latere Herjulvsnesi situm, ex habitatis
Grönlandiæ tractibus orienti
esse proximum.

ward from Herjulfsnees is Ketilsfjord, which is quite full of settlements. At the entrance of the fjord on the right hand side, is a large bay, into which fall several streams. Near this is a church, called the Church of Arós, dedicated to the Holy Cross. This church owns everything on the outside as far as Herjulfsnaes, islands and rocks, and whatever the sea throws up, and on the inside, everything as far as Petersvig. At Petersvig is a large inhabited district, called Vatsdal, near which is a large lake, two nautical miles broad, abounding in fish. Petersvig church owns the whole district of Vatsdal. Not far from this is a large monastery of canons regular, dedicated to Saint Olaus and Saint Augustine.

Item for vesten Herjulfsnes ligger Ketilsfjord ; och der er fulld bygt ; och oppaa høgre Hand, som mand indseigler i Fjorden, ligger ett stort Os, som store Ellffver løbe udi ; hos den Os stander en Kierche, som hedder Auroos Kierche, som vigt er till det hellige Kaars ; hun eyer alt ud till Herjulfsnes, Öyer, Holmer, Vragh, och allt ind til Peiters Viigh.

Item ved Peitersvig ligger en stoer Bygd, som hedder Vatnsdal. Ner den Bygd ehr edt stoertt Vand, thou Vegger Søes brett, fulltt med Fisch. Peitersvig Kierche eyger al Vatnsdalsbygd. Item end fraa den Bygd ligger edt stortt Closter, som Canonici Regulares ere udi, som vigt er thill St. Olluff och St. Augustinum. Clostered eyer

Ab occidentali latere Herjulvsnesi situs est Ketilsfjordus, totus coloniis refertus. Sinum ingredienti a dextrâ ingens ostium situm est, in quod magni fluvii se exonerant. Prope ab hoc ostio templum est, dictum templum Arosi, sacræ cruci consecratum, quod templum ab exteriori parte omnia ad Herjulvsnesum usque possidet, insulas, scopulos, marisque ejectamenta, ab interiori parte omnia ad sinum usque Petri.

Ad sinum Petri ingens tractus habitatus situs est, dictus Vatsdalus, prope quem tractum amplus lacus est, piscibus abundans, latus duo milliaria maritima. Templum Petri totum tractum Vatsdalensem possidet.

Haud procul ab hoc tractu ingens monasterium situm est, a Canonicis regularibus habitatum, Sancto Olavo et Sancto Augustino consecratum. Mo-

To it belongs all the land on the inside to the end of the fjord, and on the outside all opposite to it. Next to Ketils-fjord is Rafnsfjord, in the inner recess of which is a convent of nuns of the order of Saint Benedict. This convent possesses all inside as far as the end of the fjord, and on the outside as far as the church which is dedicated to Saint Olaus the king. The church possesses all the land on the outer side of the fjord. On the inner side are many small islands, one half of which belong to the convent, the other half to the cathedral church. These small islands abound in warm water, which, in the winter is intolerably hot, but in summer is more temperate, and can be used for

---

alt ind i Bottnen och alt ud paa den anden Side.

Item nest Ketilsfjord ligger Rafnsfjord, och langt ind udi den Fjord ligger edt Søster-Closter Ordinis Sancti Benedicti ; det Closter eger alt ind i Bottnen och ud fraa Voge Kierche, som (vigt) er till St. Olluff Konningh. Voge Kierche eger alt Land Fjorden udenfore. Ind i Fjorden ere mange Hollme, och Klostered eger alle sammen Heltten med Dombkierchen ; udi disse Hollme er meget varmbt Vand, som om Vinterren ehr saa hitt, att ingen maa komme neer, men om Sommeren ehr det vell till Made hett, saa att mand maa der baade udi, och mange fanger der Helseboed, och bliffver karsche och fanger Helseboed aff Sotter.

nasterium a parte interiori omnia ad finem sinûs, omniaque exterius ab opposito latere possidet.

Proximus Ketilsfjordo est Rafnsfjordus, in cujus interiori recessu cœnobium Sororum ordinis Sancti Benedicti situm est. Quod cœnobium a parte interiori omnia possidet ad finem usque sinûs, a parte exteriore ab templo usque Vogensi, quod Sancto regi Olavo sacrum est.

Templum Vogense omnem terram ab exteriori sinûs parte possidet. In sinu interiori multæ sunt parvæ insulæ, quarum omnium partem dimidiam cœnobium, alteram dimidiam templum cathedrale possidet. Hæ parvæ insulæ calidâ aquâ abundant, quæ hieme adeo fervent, ut nemini prope accedere fas sit ; æstate temperatæ sunt, ut lavacri usum præstent, mul-

bathing, and for the cure of many diseases. Next to this is Einarsfsjord, between which and the above-mentioned Rafnsfjord is a great property of the king's, named Foss. Here there is a splendid church dedicated to Saint Nicholas, the priests of which are appointed by the king. In the vicinity is a large lake abounding in fish, which rises with the tide of the sea, and with the rain, but when the water flows back and decreases, a great quantity of fish are left upon the sand.

On the left as you enter Einarsfjord is an arm of the sea called Thorvaldsvig, and more inward on the same side of the fjord is a promontory called Klining. Still further inwards is an inlet called Gravevig, a little inside of

---

Item der nest ligger Einarsfjord, och emellum hannem och forschreffne Rafnsfjord ligger en stoer Hoffgaard, som høerer Konningen till, och den Gard hedder Foss; och der stander en kostelig Kierche, vigt till Sanctum Nicolaum, som Konningen haffver att forlenne; och der ner ligger en stoer Fischesøe fulld med Fisch, och thaa nar stortt Vand och Regen kommer, och nar det Vand udfallder och mindsches, daa bliffver der utalig meget Fisch liggendis igen paa Sandet.

Item da mand indseyler paa venstre Hand ind udi Einarsfjord, ligger enn Vig, som hedder Thorvaldsvig, och end lenger i Fjorden ligger paa samme Side edt Nes, som hedder Klining, och end lenger ligger enn Vig,

tique sanitati restituantur et ex morbis convalescant.

Proximus huic situs est Einarsfjordus, inter quem et ante dictum Rafnsfjordum magna jacet villa principalis, quæ regi est; ei villæ nomen Foss. Hic splendidum templum stat, sancto Nicolao sacrum, cui rex sacerdotes præficit. Jacet ibi in vicinia ingens lacus, piscibus abundans, qui cum æstu marino et imbre restagnavit, aquâ refluente et decrescente magna piscium copia in arenâ remanet.

Einarsfjordum ad sinistram ingredientibus brachium maris est, dictum Thorvaldsvig; adhuc magis introrsum ad idem sinûs latus promontorium jacet, dictum Kliningus; inde magis introrsum brachium se inserit,

which is a locality called Dalr, which belongs to the
cathedral church. As you go into the fjord towards the
cathedral church, which lies in its innermost recess, there
is on the right hand a large wood belonging to the cathedral, in which all the cathedral cattle, both large and small,
are pastured. The cathedral possesses the whole of Einarsfjord,
as well as the large island that lies in front of Einarsfjord
called Rensöe, so called because in autumn many reindeer
resort thither. It is a public hunting ground for them, but
not without the bishop's permission. In this island is the
best stone for carving in all Greenland. It is of so tractable
a consistency that they make pots and cups of it, and yet so
durable that it resists injury from fire ; out of one of these

som hedder Grauevig, och fraa
Grauevig end lenger ligger en
stoer Gard, som hedder Daler,
och høer Dombkierchen till.
Och oppaa høgre Hand, som
indzeylles udi Fjorden till
Dombkierchen, som stander ind
udi Botnen, ligger en stoer
Schouff, och hører Dombkierchen till ; udi den samme
Schouff haffuer Dombkierchen
alt sitt Femett baade stordt
och smaa ; Dombkierchen eyer
alld Einars Fjord och sam-
meledes denn store Oee, som
ligger udenfore Einarsfjord, och
hedder Renøøe, saa kaldit, fordi
om Høsten løbe der utallige
Rendjuer ; der er almindelig
Vedschaff, och da iche uden
Bischopens Orloff. Och paa den
Oe chr (de) beste Talgesteen, som
paa Grönnland sees, saa nattur-
lig gode att de gjöre deraff Gry-

dictum Grauavig, intra quam
aliquanto spatio magna villa est,
dicta Dalus, templi cathedralis
possessio. Sinum ingredienti
petentique templum cathedrale
in intimo sinûs recessu situm,
a dextra est ingens sylva, ædi
cathedrali propria, in quâ sylvâ
omnia templi cathedralis pecora
magna parvaque pascuntur.
Templum cathedrale totum
Einarsfjordum possidet, item
ingentem illam insulam, quæ
Einarsfjordum præjacet, dictam
Rensöam, quod tempore autum-
nali multi eo maclides concur-
rant ; ibidem venatio communis,
neque tamen nisi permittente
episcopo. In eâdem insulâ sunt
saxa sectilia omnium quæ Grönlandia fert præstantissima, tam
sequaci materia, ut inde ollæ
et canthari conficiantur, tamque
durabili natura, ut injuriam

RUINS OF THE CHURCH AT KAKORTOK.

stones vessels are made that will hold ten or twelve hogsheads of water.

Further to the west, and in front of the mainland, is an island called Langöe, in which are eight great orchards. The cathedral church possesses the whole island, but the tithes belong to the church of Hvalsöe. Next to Einarsfjord is Hvalsöerfjord, in which is the church called Hvalsöerfjord church,[1] which owns the whole of that fjord as well as the adjoining one named Kambstadefjord. In this fjord is a royal property of great extent called Thjodhildestad. Next

der och Kander, och er saa stadig Steen, att Illden kand den iche fortere, och gjores der saa store Kander aff een Steen, som X eller XII Tonner ganger udi. Och daa vester lenger for Landet ligger en Øe, som hedder Langoe, och i den Øe ligger VIII store Bundegarde. Dombkierchen eyer alld Øen uden Thienden; Thienden ligger till Hvalsøe Kierche.

Item nest Einarsfjord ligger Hvalsøerfjord; der ligger en Kierche, som hedder Hvalsøefjords Kierche; hun eyer ald Fjorden, och saa alld Kambstadefjord, som nest ligger. Udi denne Fjord er en stoer Hoffgard, som Konningen høver till, och hedder Thjodhildestad.

ignis contemnant; ex uno tali saxo canthari, decem vel duodecim doliorum capaces, conficiuntur. Longius versus occidentem insula continentem præjacet, dicta Langöa, in qua octo grandia prædia rusticana sunt. Templum cathedrale totam insulam possidet, exceptis decimis, quæ templi Hvalsöensis sunt.

Proximus Einarsfjordo est Hvalsöerfjordus, in quo templum est, dictum Hvalsöefjordense, quod totum hunc sinum, totumque qui proxime adjacet Kambstadefjordum possidet. In hoc sinu magnum jacet prædium regium, dictum Thjodhildestadus.

---

[1] I am inclined to think that this, though not so placed by Rafn, is the famous church of Kakortok, the remains of which have been not unfrequently represented. In Bradford's noble work on the Arctic Regions, published in the present year, are beautiful photographic views of the ruins, from one of which the annexed is taken.—R. H. M.

E

to this is Erick'sfjord, at the entrance of which is an island
named Ericksöe, half of which belongs to the cathedral
church, the other half to the church of Dyrnaes. Of all
the churches in Greenland, that of Dyrnaes is the most
frequented. It stands on the left hand as you enter Ericksfjord. The church of Dyrnaes owns everything as far
as Midfjord. Midfjord stretches out from Ericksfjord
due northwest. Farther inside of Ericksfjord is the
church of Solfjall, which owns all Midfjord; still farther
inward of the fjord is the church of Leide, which owns all
up to the end of the fjord, as well as on the opposite side
as far as Burfjall. All beyond Burfjall belongs to the

Item dernest ligger Erichsfjord,
och forst i Fjorden ligger en Øe,
som hedder Eriksøe; hun hører
Hallfdellen Dombkierchen till
och Hallfdellen Dyurenes-Kier-
che till; Dyurenes Kierche ehr
denn storste Kierche Sogn, som
paa Grönnland ligger, och ligger
den samme Kierche paa Vester-
handen, som mandindseyller i
Erichsfjord. Dyurenes Kierche
eyer aldt innd udi Mittfjord;
Mittfjord schjuder ud fraa
Erichsfjord rett udi Nordvest; och ind lenger udi
Erichsfjord ligger Solefjellds
Kierche; hun eger ald Mittfjord.
Da lenger ind i Fjorden ligger
Leyder Kierche, hun eger alt
ind i Botnen och saa ud paa den
anden Side till Burfjelld; och
alldt ud fraa Burfjelld hører

Huic proximus est Eriksfjor-
dus, in cujus ostio insula quæ-
dam sita est, dicta Eriksöa,
cujus pars dimidia templo cathedrali, altera dimidia templo Dyrnesensi subjacet. Cœtuum sa-
crorum, qui in Grönlandia sunt,
templi Dyrnesensis frequentatis-
simus est, quod templum ab
sinistro latere Eriksfjordum ingredienti situm est. Templo
Dyrnesensi omnia Midfjordum
usque subjecta sunt; Midfjordus
ex Eriksfjordo recta in japygem
infunditur. Longius inde in
Eriksfjordo situm est templum
Solfjallense, cui totus Midfjordus subjectus est. In sinu
interiori longius situm est templum Leidense (curiale), cui
omnia ad finem usque sinus,
et ab adverso latere usque ad
Burfjallum subjecta sunt. Omnia, quae ab exteriori parte

cathedral church. There is situated the great settlement called Brattelid, where the comptroller usually has his residence. In departing hence one is said to go to the islands. Further westward from Langöe lie four islands named Lamböe, and Lamböe Sound, so called because it lies between Lamböe and Langöe. Inwards nearer to Ericksfjord is another sound called Fossasund. The islands just mentioned belong to the cathedral church, but Fossa Sund lies at the entrance of Ericksfjord. Northward from Ericksfjord are two arms of the sea, one called Ydrevig (outer) and the other Indrevig (inner) from their respective positions. Nearest to these on the north is Bredefjord, in which lies

Dombkierchen till. Der ligger en stoer Gard, som hedder Brattelede, som pleyer Lagmader att i boe. Nu sigges derefter at fare till Øyer. Vester lenger fran Langøe ligger fire Øer, som hedder Lambøer, och Lambøer Sund, och derfor hedder det Lambøer Sund, (fordi) det Sund ligger imellum Lambøe och Langøe. Da ind lenger till Erichsfjord ligger edt andet Sund, som hedder Fossasund. Disse forshreffne Øer høerer Dombkierchen till, och forschreffne Fossasund ligger i Indgangen till Erichsfjord.

Item der nordenfor Erichsfjord ligger thou Vigger, som hedder Ydrevig och Indrevig; thi de ligge saa till.

Item dernest norden ligger Bredefjord och i den Fjord ligger

Burfjalli sunt, templum cathedrale tenet. Ibi situm est ingens prædium, dictum Brattelida, ubi prætor domicilium habere solet. Hinc proficiscens in insulas proficisci dicitur. Longius versus occidentem ab Langöa quatuor insulæ jacent, dictæ Lamböæ, item fretum Lamböense, sic dictum, quod inter Lamböam et Langöam intercedat. Ab interiori parte propius Eriksfjordum aliud fretum situm est, dictum Fossasundum. Insulæ modo memoratæ templo cathedrali subjacent, antedictum vero Fossasundum situm est in introitu Eriksfjordi.

Boream versus ab Eriksfjordo duo maris brachia sita sunt, quorum alteri nomen Exterioris, alteri Interioris, nominibus situm exprimentibus.

His proximus a borea situs est Bredefjordus, in quo sinu

Mjöefjord. Further north is Eyrarfjord. Next to that
is Borgefjord, then Lodmunderfjord, then Isefjord, which
is the last fjord to the westward of those belonging to
the East Bygd. These islands are all frequented by the
inhabitants.

Between the east and west Bygds are twelve nautical
miles, the whole extent of which is entirely uninhabited.
In the west Bygd is a large church called Steinnaes, which
for some time was a cathedral, and a bishop's see ; but now
the Skrellings have possession of the whole west Bygd.
There are however many horses, oxen, and sheep, but all wild.
There are no men, either Christians or heathens.

Ivar Bardsen, a Greenlander, who for many years was

Mjoefjord, tha norden enger
Eirarfjord, dernest Borgerfjord,
da Lodmunderfjord, tha nest
och vesterst aff Østrebygden,
ligger Josefjord. Alle desse Øer
ehre bogde.

Item fran Osterbygd och till
Vesterbygd er en Tolt Sjoes, och
alt ubygt. Och da fram udi
Vesterbøgt stander en stoer
Kierche, som hedder Stensnes-
Kierche ; den Kierche var en
Stund Dombkierche och Bis-
chops-Sedet. Nu haffuer Skrel-
linge all Vesterbygden ud ; daa
er der noch Heste, Geder, Nod,
Faar, alt villdt och ingen Fooch,
christenn eller hedenn.

Item dette alt, som forsagt er,
sagde oss Iffver Bardsen Grönlæn
der, som var Forstander paa Bis-

Mjoefjordus jacet ; hinc longius
a borea situs est Eyrarfjordus ;
huic proximus Borgefjordus,
deinde Lodmunderfjordus, tum
Isefjordus, qui sinuum provinciæ
orientalis ad occidentem ultimus
est. Hæ omnes insulæ incolis
frequentantur.

Inter Æstbygdam et Vest-
bygdam duodecim milliaria maritima interjacent, quod totum
litoris spatium ab incolis vacu-
um est. Et protinus in Vest-
bygda stat magnum templum,
dictum Steinnesium, quod aliquanto tempore cathedrale
sedesque episcopalis fuit. Nunc
Skrelingi totum tractum occidentalem tenent ; est tamen illic
affatim equorum, boum, ovium,
quæ omnia animalia fera sunt ;
nulli homines, neque christiani, neque pagini. Ivar
Bardsonius Grönlandus, qui

procurator of Garda, the episcopal see of Greenland, informed us that he had seen all that is above described, and that he was one of those who was selected by the governor to go to the west Bygd to expel the Skrellings. When they arrived there, they found no man either Christian or heathen, but only some cattle and sheep running wild, of which they took as many as they could carry on board the ships, and returned home. The above-named Ivar Bardsen was one of them. To the north of the west Bygd is a great mountain called Hemelrachi, beyond which no man may sail without peril of his life, on account of the numerous whirlpools in that sea. Greenland abounds in silver mines, in white

---

chobsgarden i Gardum paa Grönnland udi mange Aar, att hand haffde alt dette seett, och hand var en aff dennem, som var udneffender aff Lagmanden, at fare till Vesterbygden emod de Skrelinge, att uddriffve de Schrellinge udaff Vesterbygd; och da de komme didt, da funde de ingen Mand, endten christenn eller heden, uden noget villdt Fæ och Faaer, och bespissede sig det villt Fæ och Faaer, saa meget som Schivene kunde berre, och zeylede saa der med hjemb, och forschreffne Iffver var der med.

Item da norden lenger fraa Vesterbygde ligger et stortt Fjeld, som hedder Hemelrachs Fjelld, och lenger aff end till dette Fjelld maa ingen Mand zeylle, som Liff vill behollde, for de mange Haffsvællge, som der liggo om alt Haffved.

Item udi Grönlan ehr noch

Gardorum, sedis episcopalis Grönlandiæ, procurator multos per annos fuit, nobis retulit, se omnia ante commemorata vidisse, unumque fuisse ex iis, qui a prætore delecti erant, ut in tractum occidentalem profecti Skrelingos inde expellerent. Quo cum venissent, nullum hominem, neque christianum neque paganum, invenerunt, tantummodo fera pecora et oves deprehenderunt, ex quibus quantum naves ferre poterant in has deportato domum redierunt. Unus ex his fuit Ivar supra memoratus.

Longius versus boream a provincia occidentali ingens mons Hemelrachi, ultra quem nemini, qui vitæ suæ consultum velit, navigare fas est, propter multas eas voragines, quibus totum illud mare scatet.

Grönlandia venis argentosis,

bears with red spots on their heads; in white falcons, in
whales' teeth, and in walrus' skins, and it surpasses all other
countries in producing all kinds of fish. Besides these things,
it produces marble of different colours, stone for carving,
which the fire cannot injure, and of which the Greenlanders
make pots, urns, and other vessels, holding from ten to twelve
hogsheads. There are also great numbers of reindeer. Greenland is never vexed with violent storms. A great quantity of
snow falls there; but the frost is not so severe as it is in
Iceland or Norway. On the tops of the mountains, and in the
plains below, grow fruits of the size of some kinds of apples,
of the best flavour, and there also grows wheat of the best sort.

Søllffbjerrig, hvide Björne, haff-
vendis røde Fleche, udi Hovedett,
hvide Falche, Hvalstendr, Ros-
tungsvörde, allehande Fischek-
jönn mere end udi nogen andre
Land; der er och Malmersten
allehande Lyder; ther er Thoe-
legesten, som aldrigh schader
Illd, och aff de Stene hugge de
Grönlender Potter, Gryder, Scho-
elle och saa store Kar, att udi
edt Kar ma ligge X eller XII
Thonner. Der er noch Rendyer.
Item udi Grönnland kommer
aldrigh store Stormeveder.
Item Sne kommer megen udi
Grönland; der er iche saa kalldt
som i Island eller Norge. Der
vogxer paa höye Fjellden och
nedre under de Aalldes Frugt
saa store som nogre Eble, och
goede att ede; der voxser den
best Hvede som verre maa.

albis ursis, rubris maculis capita
distinctis, albis falconibus, den-
tibus cetorum, pellibus rosma-
rorum abundat; copia omnis
piscium generis ceteras omnes
terras superat.

Eadem fert marmora diversi
coloris, saxa sectilia, igni invio-
labilia, exquibus Grönlandi ollas,
urnas, catinos et vasa, decem
aut duodecim doliorum capacia,
conficiunt.   Ibidem rangifero-
rum copia suppetit. Grönlandiam violentæ ventorum tem-
pestates   nunquam   fatigant.
Ibidem magna vis nivium deci-
dit; frigus non tam acre, quam
in Islandia aut Norvegia.   In
summis montibus et subjectis
campis proveniunt fructus cer-
torum pomorum magnitudine,
optimi saporis. Ibidem triticum
optimæ notæ crescit.

FINIS.

INDEX.

ERRATUM.

P. xvi, line 5 from bottom, for " all" read " old."

DIRECTIONS TO BINDER.

Map of the Færoe Islands to face page xv.
Zeno Map to face page xvii.
S.W. of Greenland to face page lxxxii.
Ruins of Church at Kakortok to face page 49.

For EU product safety concerns, contact us at Calle de José Abascal, 56–1°, 28003 Madrid, Spain or eugpsr@cambridge.org.

 www.ingramcontent.com/pod-product-compliance
Ingram Content Group UK Ltd.
Pitfield, Milton Keynes, MK11 3LW, UK
UKHW012345130625
459647UK00009B/534